Sustainable Frontiers offers a radically diff╵   ╵ ╵   ╵ndle change. For sustainability to become reality and not just be a politically correct buzzword, the elephant must replace the lion as the guiding spirit.
Clem Sunter, Scenario Planner and author of *21st Century Megatrends*

Wayne has woven a "wonder-full" quilt of ideas, contexts and currents on where sustainability has brought us—and could take us. Enjoyable, erudite, entertaining and enlightened.
Dr Puvan J. Selvanathan, Head, Food and Agriculture, UN Global Compact

Sustainable Frontiers describes a new and exciting path for business that truly sustains the planet and all its inhabitants. It calls the sustainable business movement to task for its failure to adopt cultures and practices that are truly restorative and sustainable. And it offers a clear set of principles to guide the transformation to sustainability that is dearly needed. My hat's off to Mr Visser for writing a timely and insightful book.
Bob Doppelt, Executive Director, The Resource Innovation Group and Transformational Resilience Program; author of *From Me to We*

If you want to sort the wheat from the chaff, and disentangle the gobbledegook from the ideas and practice that really matter, then Wayne Visser is your man—and *Sustainable Frontiers* provides a great way of accessing important insights into a world that is going to be more and more critical to future business success.
Jonathon Porritt, Founder Director, Forum for the Future; author of *The World We Made*

A book for the season—a time for doing, a time for moving ahead and not a time for endless debate and posturing. A book that provides answers to the questions that we had. A must-read for anyone interested in CSR/sustainability.
Thomas Thomas, CEO, ASEAN CSR Network

By setting out clearly the rationale of the sustainability movement, the book unlocks changes through transformational leadership and technology innovation that could play a pivotal role in reshaping corporations.
Dr Tapan Sarker, Discipline Leader, Sustainable Enterprise, Griffith University Business School

Wayne Visser combines a globally informed big-picture approach to transitioning capitalism towards a thriving future, with hundreds of great examples and stories of the transformations taking place at the edges of our mainstream corporate system. The big question, as always, is how fast can that scale in a race between declining natural carrying capacities and rapidly evolving human, social and intellectual capacities for innovation and breakthrough?
Dr Robin Wood, author of *A Leader's Guide to ThriveAbility*; Founder of the ThriveAbility Foundation

Sustainable Frontiers brings the kind of well-informed yet readable insights to sustainability that we have come to expect from Wayne Visser. This book is much more than a dry textbook; it deals with complex issues succinctly, with verve and understanding. The author is one of the few sustainability protagonists who is unencumbered by a narrow lens on the world. A truly global perspective is taken, embracing the latest developments and combining them with scholarly and wide-ranging business examples. Above all, the book is forward-looking, offering measured solutions and suggestions for the future.
Laura J. Spence, Professor of Business Ethics, Royal Holloway University of London

Wayne Visser has written a powerful and comprehensive overview of the leadership needed to navigate our times with integrity, efficiency and common sense. Here are actionable solutions for a sustainable and thriving world for all—there's no getting round it now!
Peter Merry, Chief Innovation Officer, Ubiquity University

Another must-read from one of the true thought leaders in corporate responsibility and sustainability. Never one to shy away from sharing bold, unflinching truths— including the motivations that drive individuals and corporations to pursue sustainability careers and goals—Dr Visser's *Sustainable Frontiers* outlines not only why but how we can move from programmatic efforts to truly transformational crowdsourcing and value-chain approaches.
John Friedman, author of *PR 2.0: How Digital Media Can Help You Build A Sustainable Brand*

Sustainable Frontiers, true to its title, is an out-of-the-box, transformative, holistic vision of Future Earth that takes one well beyond current concerns about Sustainability. The author's innovative concepts (e.g. CSR 2.0), extensive global experience (70 nations in 20 years), his keen grasp of digital technology's potentials, plus a pragmatic linkage of scholarly theory with business practices might well be labelled "Visserian" pathways leading business, society and the entire globe into a liveable future. "Unlocking change"—in corporate leadership, transparency, technological innovation, stakeholder relations, value integration and biocultural fitness—is the author's "golden thread" that weaves the needed solution. Listen up, students, professors, corporate leaders!
William C. Frederick, Professor Emeritus, Katz Graduate School of Business, University of Pittsburgh and author of four books

Wayne takes the reader on a journey, through the individual, business and systems approach to CSR and sustainability—and he does not miss a thing! Utilizing live case studies from across the globe of innovative approaches to addressing these complex issues, he allows the reader to reach an informed opinion of where to take a stand.
Ruby Sandhu, Lawyer, Mediator, Facilitator and Founder of RS Collaboration

Sustainable Frontiers

Unlocking Change through Business,
Leadership and Innovation

Sustainable Frontiers

Unlocking Change through Business, Leadership and Innovation

—————— WAYNE VISSER ——————

Routledge
Taylor & Francis Group

LONDON AND NEW YORK

First published 2015 by Greenleaf Publishing Limited

Published 2017 by Routledge
2 Park Square, Milton Park, Abingdon, Oxon OX14 4RN
711 Third Avenue, New York, NY 10017, USA

Routledge is an imprint of the Taylor & Francis Group, an informa business

Cover by Sadie Gornall-Jones
Stock vector illustration by surassawadee/Shutterstock.com

British Library Cataloguing in Publication Data:
A catalogue record for this book is available from the British Library.

ISBN-13: 978-1-78353-507-1 [hbk]
ISBN-13: 978-1-78353-485-2 [pbk]

Contents

Acknowledgements

My books are always a way for me to capture and share what I have learned. And I learn by researching and writing. Therefore, I would like to thank *The Guardian*, which has been publishing my writing since 2012. My chapters on sustainability leadership and enterprise reform draw on this writing especially.

I would also like to acknowledge the United Nations Environment Programme (UNEP)—including Katie Tuck and Garrette Clark—since some of the research I did for them has contributed to the chapter on technology innovation. However, none of the content is endorsed by UNEP.

I learn not only from research and writing, but also learn from people that I work with—in Cambridge and elsewhere—and those who I interact with in countries all around the world, who constantly challenge my thinking.

Therefore, I would like to thank my colleagues at Kaleidoscope Futures—including Scott Walker, Amos Doornbos, Ileana Magureanu, Azadeh Ardakani and Nicola Dee—in particular for their contribution to the chapters on corporate transparency, stakeholder engagement and technology innovation.

Likewise, my gratitude goes to the team at the University of Cambridge Institute for Sustainability Leadership—including Polly Courtice, Theo Hacking, Louise Driffill and others—in particular for their contribution to my thinking on sustainability leadership.

And to the Gordon Institute of Business Science (GIBS) in South Africa, where I hold my Transnet Chair in Sustainable Business—including Claire Thwait, Morris Mthombeni, Tasmia Ismail and Bongiwe Ramaboea—I appreciate the ongoing support and passion for pushing sustainable frontiers in Africa.

Finally, to my amazing wife, Indira Kartallozi, who inspires me daily with her work to support vulnerable families, migrants and refugees through Chrysalis Family Futures, as well as her unfailing encouragement in the sustainability work that I do and that, increasingly and happily, we are doing together.

Introduction: the art of letting go

Exploring future frontiers means letting go of the past

I was delighted to be reminded recently of a little story in the prologue to Richard Bach's (1977) inspiring book, *Illusions: The Adventures of a Reluctant Messiah*. Here is how it goes:

> Once there lived a village of creatures along the bottom of a great crystal river. The current of the river swept silently over them all—young and old, rich and poor, good and evil, the current going its own way, knowing only its own crystal self. Each creature in its own manner clung tightly to the twigs and rocks of the river bottom, for clinging was their way of life, and resisting the current what each had learned from birth.
>
> But one creature said at last, "I am tired of clinging. Though I cannot see it with my eyes, I trust that the current knows where it is going. I shall let go, and let it take me where it will. Clinging, I shall die of boredom." The other creatures laughed and said, "Fool! Let go, and that current you worship will throw you tumbled and smashed across the rocks, and you will die quicker than boredom!"
>
> But the one heeded them not, and taking a breath, did let go, and at once was tumbled and smashed by the current across the rocks. Yet in time, as the creature refused to cling again, the current lifted him free from the bottom, and he was bruised and hurt no more.

I share this little story extract, because it speaks so exactly to the theme of this book, which is pursuing the frontiers of sustainability by unlocking change. So much of making a successful transition to a more sustainable future (which is by no means certain) depends on *letting go*.

In the pages that follow, we will explore how we must find ways to let go of an industrial system that has served us well, but is no longer fit for purpose. We will need to let go of old styles of leadership and outdated models of business, high-impact lifestyles and selfish values. We must learn to let go of cherished ideologies that are causing destruction and beliefs about ways to tackle problems that are failing to resolve crises.

It is no wonder that we are scared to let go. Many of us are comfortable clinging to our consumptive habits and selfish behaviours. Besides, the future is uncertain—and our greatest fear as humans is a fear of the unknown. We would rather trust (and fight to protect) the present we know than gamble on the future we don't know.

And yet, as academic Jared Diamond (2005) has documented in *Collapse*, civilizations that fail to change are civilizations that ultimately fall. Furthermore, historian Arnold Toynbee (1988) points out that the decline of civilizations starts with the failure to open the public and political mind to new possibilities. People become trapped in a paradigm—literally, a pattern of thinking—and are closed to a different, emergent world-view, despite mounting evidence supporting the new reality.

If we are to reach sustainable frontiers, therefore, it must begin with changing our collective minds—and only then will we change our collective behaviour. How we accomplish such a global mind-shift is the subject of this book. And it starts by admitting that those of us at the vanguard of the sustainability revolution also have to change. We will also have to let go of cherished beliefs and strategies that are not working—starting with the way we communicate our vital, life-saving mission.

The sustainability movement faces extinction—what could save it?

We all want to change the world, but where to begin? Maybe a good start would be getting as far away from sustainability as possible. If you are already in its clutches, don't despair: it's not too late to turn around, walk away and never look back. Forget you ever heard the "S-word" and take a vow of silence never to speak it again. Once you've done that, you might consider joining a tech company (infotech, biotech, cleantech—it doesn't matter which; they will all be indistinguishable soon). I'm betting that would be a good way to kick-start your world-changing mission.

I say this after 20 years as a professional in sustainability (capital S if you're a devotee), which I've discovered to be many things, but certainly not an effective strategy for change—at least, not yet. The reason is fairly simple: the essential idea of sustainability—that we must endure, perpetuate, hold on to the past and drag it into the future—is about as exciting as watching lettuce wilt under the midday sun. As Michael Braungart, co-author of *Cradle to Cradle* (Braungart and McDonough, 2008), likes to say: "sustainability is boring".

I imagine your expressions of shock and horror, but it's true. Sustainability has won many battles—for best-new-jargon-inventor, for most-likely-to-make-you-feel-good—but has lost the war for the hearts and minds of the people. It has pinned its colours to the mast of scarcity and survival, when most of the world is far more interested in prosperity and thriving. I'd go so far as to say that the sustainability movement has failed to understand what it means to be human.

Let me explain. As human beings, our lives are all about change—about growth and development. At best, life is about making things better. Even as a civilization, we're all about evolution, although we prefer to call it progress. Now, as it happens, sustainability "wonks" believe that they are all about Progress with a capital P. Unfortunately, the rest of the world remains unconvinced.

Sustainability is like a geeky, pimply teenager who has come to our party, turned off the music and told us that we would really be much happier if we stopped having so much darn fun! The key to having a good time, declares our party pooper, is to practise a lot more self-restraint. All those on board the austerity train, say "Hell, yeah!" … What, no one?

Make no mistake; if we are to survive (let alone thrive), the world is going to *have* to change—dramatically, radically and irreversibly. The question is: how will it happen? In this book, I'll be digging into the nature of change and what role we play as leaders in making it happen—in our societies, our organizations and as individuals. And when change does turn our lives upside down (as it will), how can we become more resilient?

To begin, let me plant a seminal idea, which is that change is all about connection. In other words, connectivity is the underlying catalyst for change.

We are living proof of this. The first neurons in our brains, called predecessors, are in place 31 days after fertilization. In the early stages of a foetus's brain development, 250,000 neurons are added every minute, and, by the time a baby is born, there are about 100 billion neurons, which remain roughly constant through life. Learning only happens when synapses are formed: they connect the neurons to each other. At birth, the number of synapses per neuron is about 2,500; by age two or three, it has risen to 15,000 and some neurons later develop up to 50,000 connections each.

Hence, the dramatic changes in the early years of a child's life—all those remarkable feats of learning and development—are due to increasing connectivity, or, as scientists like to call it, complexity. And we see this same pattern at work in society. The first computer, Charles Babbage's analytical machine of 1837, would have had the equivalent of 675 bytes of memory. By comparison, according to Cisco, between 1984 and 2012, the Internet generated 1.2 zettabytes of data—that's 1.2 with 20 zeros after it.

The point is that scaling the number of networked relationships is at the heart of almost all change, including biological and social evolution. My contention is that, if we wish to save the sustainability movement from an ironic fate of extinction, we will have to get much smarter about change: better at riding the waves of science and technology, better at becoming intelligently connected, and better at designing change efforts that align with evolutionary dynamics.

For this reason, "unlocking change" is the golden thread that runs through this book. In the chapters to follow, we will explore how to unlock change through transformational leadership, enterprise reform, technology innovation, corporate transparency, stakeholder engagement, integrated value and future-fitness. So buckle up, it's going to be an exciting ride! (and we'll skip the farm of withering lettuce).

1
Unlocking change through transformational leadership

Why today's crisis of leadership is tomorrow's opportunity

> You have lost your reason and taken the wrong path. You have taken lies for truth, and hideousness for beauty ... I marvel at you who exchange heaven for earth.

These words by author Anton Chekhov (1995) were not written about our contemporary business leaders, but they might just as well have been. I will be arguing in this chapter that we desperately need transformational leadership in order to advance the frontier of sustainability. But before we reach for those heady heights, let us revisit the muddy swamps of calamitous leadership—of catastrophic, cancerous, disastrous, pestilential, cataclysmic leadership. Is there any other way to describe the business leadership that led us all, Pied Piper-like, into the 2008 global financial crisis—the aftershock of which is still being felt and the burden of which weigh heavy on generations to come?

This was a crisis ushered in while leading companies around the world—and their celebrated CEOs—all seemed to be happily chanting "greed is good" in unison. That mantra, of course, belongs to the fictional Wall Street character, Gordon Gekko, but apparently truth is stranger than fiction. Our MBA-trained leaders all seemed to agree with Gekko, when he said: "Greed is right, greed works. Greed clarifies, cuts through, and captures the essence of the evolutionary spirit. Greed, in all of its forms—greed for life, for money, for love, knowledge—has marked the upward surge of mankind."

Am I being too melodramatic? Maybe, or maybe not. In my co-authored book *Beyond Reasonable Greed* (Visser and Sunter, 2002), we attributed the phenomenon of unreasonable corporate greed at the turn of the century to boards "being collectively swept along by the prevailing paradigm of success which is purely financial". However, we added the following rider: "In light of Enron's failure, this judgement may be overly kind and more cases of dodgy accounting, inflated profits and insider trading by the board may pop up in Corporate America and Corporate Europe."

And of course, since publication, they did pop up, like a popping popcorn poppathon—starting with WorldCom, but also later extending to other corporate heavyweights, such as Lehman Brothers. As a result, big business is under the whip like never before from the public and politicians alike. And the finance profession, in particular, is feeling very uncomfortable under the harsh interrogative spotlight. However, if the response to all the accounting irregularities and other misdemeanours is merely to throw a few CEOs in jail and threaten the rest with a long prison sentence unless they check the figures personally, a great opportunity for real transformation will be lost.

As business and the financial services industry begins to respond to the rising tide of international scrutiny, the word "corporate governance" is on everybody's lips. But the critics remain sceptical, maybe justifiably so. If wave after wave of corporate scandals are revealing anything, it is that corporate governance is sometimes not worth the paper it is written on. If the people involved in implementing corporate governance do not have their hearts in the right place and if they are just going through the motions, the process becomes a charade.

You can have all the non-executive chairpersons, non-executive directors, board committees and external auditors you like, but things will go hideously wrong if ceremony has replaced substance and cynicism is the order of the day. Some non-executive directors sit on so many boards that it is physically impossible for them to exercise their fiduciary responsibilities properly—let alone wider social responsibilities.

Worse still is a situation where the Chairman and CEO are one and the same person and he (it still almost always is a "he") has managed to load the board with his buddies. If things go right, they are the first to congratulate him and approve a handsome bonus. If things go wrong, they are the last to ask the tough questions needed to expose malpractice. They would prefer to have the wool pulled firmly over their eyes even though ignorance is no excuse in terms of the law.

Seeking a reformation in business

So let's be clear about what we mean by transformational leadership. Rather than implementing a smattering of short-term corporate governance fixes (which are necessary, but not sufficient), what is required is nothing short of a Reformation in business, along the same lines as the one precipitated by Martin Luther in 1517. On October 31 of that year, he wrote an attack on the sale of indulgences (remissions of punishment for sin) in 95 theses, which he nailed to a church door. His basic point was that the Church had become too interested in enriching itself at the expense of its true mission of providing spiritual leadership. It had lost the support of the population at large with its mercenary practices and obsession with grandeur and wealth.

In exactly the same way, the modern corporate world has lost the confidence of the public. The high priests of business—the board of directors—are perceived as just another example of a group of privileged people driven by unreasonable greed and feathering their own nests. The customers and shareholders come a poor second and other stakeholders trail even further behind. The modern equivalent of indulgences is an astronomical salary, a large wad of share options and a corporate jet. And the modern equivalent of the flowery and unintelligible prayers which the Church used to recite in order to extract its indulgences from the peasantry is the purple prose and lofty sentiments expressed by companies in their mission statement, combined with a set of accounts that only the initiated can understand.

So reform is critical for business to restore its reputation, particularly as its presence in society rivals that of the Church in the 16th century. Hence, we see business needing to establish a new and broader role for itself, in keeping with modern times, rather than going back to the old one. Another word for this type of change is "shapeshifting"—liberating ourselves from the old form that defined and constrained us in the past and morphing into a completely new being, with new characteristics and potential for the future. And despite my cheeky dismissal of the "S-word" in the Introduction, I still believe that sustainability *can be* the catalyst which helps us in the process of shapeshifting.

Unfortunately, sustainability is almost a cliché now. Nevertheless, the idea behind it remains a powerful source of inspiration and is responsible for an umbrella movement encompassing as diverse a group as you can imagine. They all share one thing in common: an interest in improving human well-being by seeking a proper balance between social, economic and environmental change.

Most fundamentally, sustainability is about surviving and thriving, by finding a proper balance between economic, social and environmental development. No one of these three elements of the so-called "triple bottom line" can be pursued relentlessly at the expense of the others, or else the whole system collapses. Sadly, at the moment, there is widespread evidence that we are out of balance and that, despite economic advances (and sometimes because of them), our ecological and social systems are breaking down. We are pursuing unsustainable development.

If you are reading this book, you probably don't need convincing of this fact. So figures should suffice to make the point. Since 1970, the expansion of our industrial economies and upgrading of our consumerist lifestyles have already resulted in vertebrate populations by over 50%, with species extinction occurring at a rate 100–1,000 times faster than the natural background rate. This is ecologically unsustainable.

At the same time, the gaps between rich and poor—and between CEO packages and workers' wages—have all widened in the past 50 years. This is socially unsustainable. Furthermore, corruption remains unresolved, with one in four people around the world having to pay a bribe for public services. Meanwhile, many countries have mortgaged the next generation's future to indebtedness in an attempt to recover from the 2008 global financial crisis. This is economically unsustainable.

Trading in business fangs for tusks

These unsustainable trends, many of them perpetuated by business, suggest that the very mode of modern business and the economy lies at the heart of the problem. To use an analogy, today the majority of business embodies the characteristics of a lion—an impressive predator. Let's take this metaphor for a walk and see where it leads us.

Like lions, companies act like competitive hunters in the marketplace, looking to dominate the economic plains, thereby gaining more power and wealth for the board of directors. Not surprisingly, financial measures of success are automatically given a higher priority than impacts on local communities or the natural environment. Lionlike boards will argue that turning themselves into fat cats will somehow miraculously "trickle down" to benefit society as a whole, despite growing evidence to the contrary. All the other animals of the wild are not convinced!

By contrast (if you will indulge the wildlife metaphor a little longer), the future calls for different strengths, such as those displayed by the mighty elephant—a wise leader. They are masters of survival and adaptation, and live largely in co-operative harmony with their fellow creatures. Elephants are organized in matriarchal herds, which display highly developed social tendencies and sophisticated communication abilities (including the use of infrasound). They are extremely intelligent creatures, but also display sensitive emotions, such as affection and grief. Most of all, these gentle giants inspire all who encounter them.

There are seven critical dimensions in which shapeshifting needs to occur in order to create sustainable companies. These deal with values, vision, work, governance, relationships, communication and services. Looking at our current crisis of leadership, we have to re-examine corporate governance. But governance is not a word that lions like much. It smacks too much of giving away power. Or sharing supper. Lion directors prefer the freedom of making all their decisions in secret councils or while they're on the run, with no justification needed and no recourse back to them. In other words, if the lion king has his way, business is a monarchy, not a democracy.

So transformational leadership means shapeshifting that goes beyond putting corporate governance ticks into boxes. At the end of the day, it is about values and behaviour. Companies that perpetuate the widening gap between rich and poor in their own payroll profile are always going to fall into the lions' camp. Companies that persist in managing from the top down will never turn their fangs into tusks. And companies that only create partnerships that benefit themselves may learn to purr, but they will never lose their roar.

Elephant-like leaders, on the other hand, embrace the principles and practices of good governance with passion. They implement governance at a practical level, including shapeshifting in at least three areas: company incentive systems, decision-making processes and communication methods.

Shifting to return on stakeholder value

I don't believe this shapeshifting is simply a nice thing to do. To survive in the sustainability era, companies will *have to* move beyond their aggressive, competitive tendencies. They will need to learn to be not only sociable, but genuinely concerned about the perspectives and wellbeing of all of their stakeholders. Of course, this is not a new idea—years ago already, Barry Nalebuff and Adam Brandenburger, in their book of the same title, called this transition *Co-opetition* (Nalebuff and Brandenburger, 1996), while David Wheeler and Maria Sillanpää talked about *The Stakeholder Corporation* (Wheeler and Sillanpää, 1997).

Companies ignore this trend at their own peril. Stakeholders, if maltreated, can bite back and even the most macho multinational lions can find themselves bleeding. Transparency is key. However, too many companies have grown accustomed to speaking to stakeholders only on a "need to know" basis—telling whom they want, what they want, when they want. Usually, this "communication" coincides with a time when the company needs something from its stakeholders, such as support (or the absence of visible protest) to proceed with a new development. There is no shortage of lion companies who mistake "telling" for "dialogue" and get backchat from angry stakeholders as a result.

Fortunately, the next generation of corporate elephant wannabes can choose the easier route of following in the footsteps of the elephant pioneers that have gone before them—such as the Body Shop's values reporting, Sbn Bank's ethical accounting process, Skandia's intellectual capital reporting, Electrolux's environmental reporting, or Puma's environmental profit and loss accounts.

There are also numerous do-it-yourself guides that have emerged over the years, such as the Accountability 1000 standard on social and ethical accounting, auditing and reporting and the Global Reporting Initiative's Sustainability Reporting Guidelines. Beyond these basic frameworks, technology-enabled interactive stakeholder feedback and real-time online public reporting on the web are already well advanced and is a theme we revisit in Chapters 4 and 5.

Our comparison of lion versus elephant companies—although a playful metaphor—offers a serious glimpse of the alternative landscapes for business that may emerge over the coming decades. These are encapsulated in two contrasting scenarios, which were explored in more detail in *Beyond Reasonable Greed* (Visser and Sunter, 2002).

"Oases in the Desert" is where the corporate lions continue to rule, but their kingdoms are increasingly restricted by their own destructive behaviour and popular discontent. "Plains of the Serengeti", on the other hand, is where companies shapeshift into elephants that strive for a proper balance between co-operation and competition and a continuing diversity of species, large and small, strong and weak.

What is certain is that our incumbent global cadre of executive leadership, along with business as a whole, is being forced to shapeshift, whether it likes it or not. And those that have the foresight to change fundamentally are more likely to remain a "going concern"—in other words, to survive and thrive—which is, ultimately, what sustainability means.

Systems change is a multiplayer game

But shapeshifting is difficult. That's because, when it comes to sustainability, we are actually talking about changing a vastly complex system—encompassing economic, social, cultural and even ethical elements. As a result, it takes a complex mix of different players to bring about lasting change. Allow me to illustrate with the example of climate change.

If Shakespeare was right that "all the world's a stage", then consider this cast of characters: Svante Arrhenius, Al Gore, Franny Armstrong, Inez Fung, Mercedes Bustamante and Colin Beavan. Now imagine the stage is set with a few props—the IPCC (Intergovernmental Panel on Climate Change), the EU Emissions Trading Scheme (EU ETS) and the Copenhagen Accord. Finally, weave in some plot twists, such as Hurricane Katrina, Chinese solar subsidies and Fukushima.

We now have all the ingredients for an intriguing play about climate change—or, to be more precise, a story about how whole systems change happens.

Let's begin with the individuals. Each represents a different type of person that is needed for societal change to be effective. Svante Arrhenius, the Swedish scientist who discovered the greenhouse effect in 1896 and linked it to fossil fuels, is typical of what we might call a genius heretic, someone who changes our paradigm, or the way we see the world.

Al Gore, former US vice president and star of *An Inconvenient Truth* (Gore, 2007), might be regarded as an iconic leader, someone who uses charisma to communicate ideas and persuade us to change. Franny Armstrong, on the other hand, with documentaries such as *McLibel* and *The Age of Stupid*, as well as her 10:10 climate campaign, is more like a freedom fighter.

So here we have three cast members and three different kinds of change agency—paradigmatic, charismatic and activist. Each individual is fairly high profile and offers the possibility of bringing about relatively rapid transformation, using ideas, persuasion and action. So how are next three individuals different?

Ines Fung is a professor of atmospheric science at the University of California, Berkley, who has been working on climate change ever since she won the MIT Rossby Award for outstanding thesis of the year in 1971. She is what we could call a systematic scientist, patiently and persistently gathering evidence how things fit together.

Mercedes Bustamante is a director in the Ministry of Science, Technology and Innovation in Brazil and co-ordinator/lead author of the fifth IPCC assessment report on mitigation. Her work is all about finding leverage points to change behaviour in society—and especially in agriculture and forestry—so that we can prevent dangerous climate change.

Colin Beavan is neither scientist nor politician. However, he does do experiments. He is most well known for *No Impact Man* (Beavan, 2011), a documentary account of his attempt to live in New York City for one year with as close to zero environmental impact as possible.

Again, we have three individuals, all advocating different pathways to change—what I call Cartesian, Newtonian and Gandhian strategies. They are typically not high-profile people and the process of change is much slower, but they form essential spokes in the wheel of systems change.

Now what of our props and plots? The IPCC also represents a relatively gradual change strategy, but operates at a collective level using the principle of consensus. The EU ETS uses a different mechanism, creating price signals as incentives for behaviour change.

Meanwhile, the 2009 Copenhagen Accord, while disappointing to many, may still turn out to be the tipping point when all the world's major nations—including developed, emerging and developing countries—finally agreed that deep cuts in global emissions are needed to avoid catastrophic climate change.

These three types of change—consensual, incentivized and pivotal—are slow societal processes that help to build the momentum towards more dramatic change. Our final trio represents revolutionary change, with catastrophic events such as Hurricane Katrina, combining with rapid growth trends, such as the way massive Chinese government subsidies have halved solar panel costs since 2010.

We also have butterfly effects, things we could not have predicted, such as Germany's policy response to the 2011 Fukushima nuclear disaster, putting it on a fast track to renewable energy. We can call these three types of change cataclysmic, exponential and chaotic.

So, taken together, what does it mean? By recognizing the different types of leader needed and the dynamics on the wheel of systems change, we start to see how shifts occur in society. At any one time, there needs to be activity in all four change triptychs—let's call them invention, intention, evolution and revolution—which is what appears to be happening already with climate change.

We know the story of a transition to a low-carbon future is far from an end. If it were a three-act play, we're undoubtedly still in Act 1. Yet it is one of the issues that have caused the most disruptive change to society in recent decades and—as the fifth IPCC assessment report confirms—it will probably get worse before it gets better.

The bottom line is that we are gambling with our climate future, but we can still spread our bets. If we want real transformation in society—by choosing a plus two-degree rather than a plus six-degree world—our best chance is to keep spinning the wheel of systems change.

Big beliefs, blue skies, burning platforms and baby steps

So far, I've been banging on about "changing the world"—in other words, big systems change—but let's be honest, for most of us, that is a bit like shooting for the stars. In practice, the moon we're most likely to hit is changing our own organizations. Easy to say, hard to do. If there is one reason why organizational change fails, it's because we underestimate resistance to change. As Hunter Lovins once told me, "Only a baby with a wet diaper wants changing, and even then, it cries throughout the process."

Resistance to change comes from inertia—and inertia happens because, as Bob Doppelt, author of *From Me to We* (Doppelt, 2012), puts it, change is like an iceberg. It is futile to keep pushing against what is above the surface—the things we can see and control directly, such as rules, policies and procedures. Shifting the volume and weight of what lies below the surface—our habits, attitudes, beliefs and values—is the real secret to making change happen.

Unfortunately, this requires the intrinsic drivers of human behaviour to be rewired, which is what makes it so much more difficult. And yet, when we succeed, the scale and speed of change can be profound. Turning carpet company Interface into the first truly restorative business on the planet began with founder Ray Anderson's "spear in the chest" revelation. Changing his world-view was the first step to changing his organization.

Change was possible because Anderson was able to combine decades of experience as an industry leader with a "fire in the belly" that came from his conversion to a new belief system. And, as with Steve Jobs, if a leader has true conviction, he or she can create a "reality distortion field" in which others get swept up in the cause.

Sadly, these missionary-type leaders with their big beliefs are about as common as Greenpeace activists championing the cause of oil companies. Most organizations have to rely on three other strategies to overcome inertia: burning platforms, blue skies and baby steps.

Let's start with baby steps, because this is usually the easiest strategy. Most organizations do not need much persuasion to commission a pilot facility, construct a demonstration project or develop a showcase product, especially with the giddy prospect of good PR spin. In fact, sustainability reports are practically burping with all the "low-hanging fruit" that these companies have gorged themselves on.

The reason these baby steps for sustainability have never become giant leaps for society is because there is no real incentive to stride out. For that, we need the other two strategies, starting with blue skies. The fact is, as humans, we are always "chasing the blue". But first we have to be convinced that where we are going is sunnier. Yet, for most people in most parts of the world—as crazy as it seems—we don't believe that a sustainable future is necessarily a better future.

Veteran environmentalist, Jonathon Porritt, is hoping he can still change our minds. His book, *The World We Made* (Porritt, 2013), sketches a vision of what he calls a genuinely sustainable world in 2050 and why it is so much better than today. It's a change management tactic that we could all learn from—the kind of thinking that inspired Elon Musk to invent Tesla Motors. Until then, nobody believed that electric cars could be not only green, but fast and cool too.

A blue skies strategy means being willing to take a risk as a leader and to set big hairy audacious goals. Whether it is Unilever's plan to double in size, while reducing its environmental footprint and helping a billion people out of poverty, or Google's ambition to make all the world's knowledge free and accessible, blue-sky leaders know that we are only inspired by reaching for an impossible dream. That's why we desperately need more Apollo-like sustainability missions that the public can get genuinely excited about.

The combination of big beliefs, baby steps and blue-sky strategies will almost certainly get us moving forward, but if we want a pace to match the urgency of our global challenges, organizations need a burning platform. Someone else's burning platform—HIV/Aids in South Africa, Amazon destruction in Brazil, or corruption in Russia—won't do the trick. Impacts that are far away, or in the future, are like smouldering fires in the distance: noteworthy but not action-worthy. People need to feel the heat: directly, personally, here and now. For organizations and leaders, that might mean lighting a few fires.

So if you're trying to make change happen in your organization, use burning platforms to create the urgency for change, blue skies to create the reasons to change, baby steps to create the momentum for change, and big beliefs to sustain the energy for change.

Finding your inner sustainability superhero

Unlocking change, however, is not only about what you do, but also who you are; or more specifically, whether you are tapped into your own power.

Have you ever wondered why do we do it? The sustainability hokey cokey, I mean. Most of us—whether we are sustainability professionals, academics, consultants, students, activists or wannabes—could have pursued different career paths. For my sins, having studied marketing, I could have become a spin doctor or an adman. So what makes us choose sustainability instead?

My research on the subject, which is written up in more detail in my book *Making a Difference* (Visser, 2008), shows that there are deep psychological—even existential—reasons why we "do" sustainability. And you may be surprised to know that it is not because we want to save the world, or because we care about people, or even because we want to make a difference. At least, not directly. The real reason is because it gives us personal satisfaction—not of the sugar rush or warm cuddly variety, but of the purpose-inspired, life satisfaction kind.

If we dig a bit deeper, we find that six motivational forces drive our work in sustainability. First, it allows us to feel that our work is aligned to our personal values, whether these are faith-based or humanistic. Second, we find the work stimulating. Sustainability is a bit like chess—it is complex, dynamic and challenging, like an ultimate earth-puzzle that needs solving. Most sustainability enthusiasts share these two drivers.

The other four drivers tend to be distributed across the sustainability tribe. Some find meaning in giving specialist input, while others prefer empowering people. Some are motivated to come up with effective strategies, while others feel most satisfied if they are making a contribution to society.

These drivers translate into a set of sustainability leader archetypes— think of them as our very own Fantastic Four, namely: experts, facilitators, catalysts and activists. Each represents a different kind of sustainability change agent.

- **Sustainability experts** tend to be focused on the details of a particular issue, with a deep knowledge and understanding, often of a technical or scientific nature. They like working on projects, designing systems and being consulted for their expertise. Their satisfaction comes from continuous learning and self-development. They are most frustrated by the failure of others to be persuaded by the compelling evidence, or to implement systems as they were designed.

- **Sustainability facilitators** are most concerned with using their knowledge to empower others to act, using their strong people skills to make change happen. They like working with teams, delivering training and giving coaching. Their satisfaction is in seeing changes in people's understanding, work or careers. They become frustrated when individuals let the team down, or when those in power do not allow enthusiastic groups to act.

- **Sustainability catalysts** enjoy the challenge of shifting an organization in a new direction, using their political skills of persuasion to change strategies. They like working with leadership teams and articulating the business case for sustainability. They are often pragmatic visionaries and are frustrated when top management fails to see—and more importantly, to act on—the opportunities and risks facing the organization.

- **Sustainability activists** are typically passionate about macro-level issues and their impacts on society or the planet as a whole, using their strong feelings about justice to motivate their actions. Their satisfaction comes from challenging the status quo, questioning those in power and articulating an idealistic vision of a better future. They tend to be great networkers and are mainly frustrated by the apathy of others in the face of urgent crises.

As you reflect on what type of sustainability superhero you may be, I expect all four will resonate to a greater or lesser extent. This is because we are composite beings when it comes to making sustainability change happen. But we do gravitate more strongly to one archetype, based on what gives us the deepest personal satisfaction. And there are good reasons why you should know which cape and tights fits you best.

Aligning with your inner superhero means embracing a mode of action in which you are most professionally effective and purpose-inspired. It allows you to check that your formal role, or the direction of your career, is consistent with your archetype—the mask must fit the cape and tights. And it encourages you to consciously put together teams with a balance of experts, facilitators, catalysts and activists—the ideal earth-crime fighting force.

So it is not enough that all change begins with individual leaders. For change to be sustained and transformational—for sustainability to be a force for good in the world, and to save the Earth from humans—we need the joint efforts of the Fantastic Four, each with their particular superpowers: knowledge for the experts, collaboration for the facilitators, imagination for the catalysts, and compassion for the activists.

Overcoming the barriers to sustainable change

In practice, even superheroes have to battle to make change happen. In 2014, *The Guardian* asked leaders with responsibility for driving sustainability within their business to identify the key barriers to sustainable change. Some 60% of those surveyed said that sustainability is perceived as a long-term issue, so only 27% believe they will make an impact on the agenda in the short term. *The Guardian* then asked me—and a number of other experts—to give their advice on how to overcome such barriers and unlock change. Here are some of my top tips.

Overcoming short-termism

The first step is to challenge the prevailing wisdom. If only a quarter of your peers believe sustainability will have a material impact on business performance in the short term, focus on the contradictory evidence. Start collecting cases, facts and figures that show how financially significant sustainability can be. No doubt when BP lost 50% of its share value in 50 days after the Deep Water Horizon spill or when Starbucks faced boycotts over perceived tax avoidance in the UK, these were material impacts.

The second step is to widen the scope of sustainability. Too many companies still understand sustainability only to be concerned with environmental issues, or with what a sustainability department is responsible for. However, when sustainability is recast as being fundamentally about the way a company does business—including how it recruits and retains talent, ensures security of resource supplies, and maintains customer satisfaction and good stakeholder relations—it becomes more difficult to argue that these have a marginal impact.

The third step is to change the market pressures for short-termism. In practice, this means identifying and promoting actions that question shareholder supremacy and financial speculation. Examples include Unilever's refusal to disclose quarterly performance, Warren Buffet's long-term investment philosophy, the global trend of socially responsible investment, and Puma's inclusion of externality costs through its Environmental Profit and Loss accounts.

Bridging the trust gap

Another barrier to sustainable change is the trust gap. Trust comes from investing in long-term relationships, rather than attempting to buy positive opinions through one-off sponsorships and charitable activities.

There are three main reasons why companies lose the trust of the stakeholders. The first is that they overpromise and under-deliver. Typically, PR departments create an inflated image of the company's sustainability credentials, while actual performance lags far behind. Hence, companies have to ground their claims in evidence and show that they are willing to invest in making real changes.

The second reason is that companies tend to be inconsistent in their behaviour. A sustainability or public affairs department may do good work with the community on the one hand, while the procurement department rides roughshod over small suppliers or the HR department cuts jobs or the finance function disinvests from a local area. Only if there is a genuine strategic commitment to sustainability from the top is this likely to change.

The third reason is that companies are perceived as having a narrow, profit-driven self-interest. Stakeholders remain sceptical of their motives and commitment to societal improvement—and rightly so. The only way to overcome this is for companies to commit to bold strategic social and environmental goals, such as Interface's Mission Zero (achieving zero environmental impact by 2020), and not to waver when the going gets tough. Aligned to this is making long-term commitments of three to five years, or even longer, to their cross-sector partners.

Bringing financial and middle managers on board

Another barrier to change is lack of support from key functions or levels in the organization, such as the finance department or middle managers. The first challenge is one of translation. Sustainability has to be translated into the language of the business or sector, and made relevant for the functional areas of the business. Hence, what does sustainability mean for the finance department?

It means examining impacts on contingent liabilities, intangible assets, investor confidence, audit and assurance procedures and corporate governance. The "S-word" does not even need to be mentioned. The second challenge is to change the way in which managers are rewarded. This is the biggest motivator of behaviour for middle management.

Hence, unless sustainability is built into the company's compensation schemes—including its performance appraisal, bonus payment, and career advancement mechanisms—we cannot expect middle managers to align their attitudes and actions behind sustainability goals.

The third challenge is more fundamental, which is to change the culture of the corporation. This comes from the leaders being consistent role models and putting their money where their mouths are. In other words, they cannot be spouting rhetoric about sustainability, or supply chain ethics, for example, while putting managers under pressure to go for maximum growth or the lowest cost suppliers.

Only when middle managers and financial pundits really believe that the company's mission has changed—and see public goodwill for their leadership on these issues—will they start to feel proud of their organization's sustainability efforts, and become its biggest champion.

Seven ways to test if your leader is fit for the future

At this point, you may be thinking: that's all very well, but unless the C-suite is on board with sustainability, all these efforts are bound to fail. You are right, of course. So let's look at what makes a genuine sustainability leader—those pioneers who understand the seriousness of the crises we face and are prepared to challenge convention and take bold remedial action.

In research that I led at the University of Cambridge Institute for Sustainability Leadership, we found that there are a number of characteristics (traits, styles, skills and knowledge) that distinguish sustainability leaders from their peers. The research is written up in more detail in an academic paper (Visser and Courtice, 2011), but let me distil the essence into seven key characteristics.

1. **Systemic, interdisciplinary understanding**: José Lopez, Executive Vice President Nestlé SA, Responsible for Operations, insists that "one of the elements that will really get us going in this sustainability fight is the elimination of the root cause for unsustainable behaviour, unsustainable business morals, unsustainable practices" (Lopez, 2010). Hence, we observe that sustainability leaders are able to think systemically, to see interconnections and to bridge silos. As Jeff Immelt (2007), CEO of General Electric, put it, "The most important thing I've learned since becoming CEO is context. It's how your company fits in with the world and how you respond to it."

2. **Emotional intelligence and a caring attitude**: Ian Cheshire, former CEO of B&Q owner Kingfisher, which has been a pioneer on sustainability for many years, believes that "real leadership is about greater and greater self-awareness and being more and more authentically yourself. The humility to listen and be aware as opposed to being on broadcast and an egomaniac, which I think is the traditional model of CEOs" (Cheshire, 2010). Jan Muehlfeit, Chairman of Microsoft Europe, agrees: "As a leader for the future, you have to motivate hearts—it takes real inspiration" (Muehlfeit, 2010).

3. **Values orientation that shapes culture**: Anurag Gupta, founder and CEO of A Little World, a micro-banking company in India that uses mobile phones to achieve financial inclusion, has a mission to "touch a billion people through innovative technologies

and alliances at the bottom of the pyramid for delivering multiple financial services at the lowest cost through mainstream financial institutions". Yet Gupta is not a banker. He started out working in the remote villages of India as a "barefoot architect", helping to design earthquake-resistant houses. Sustainability leaders will always find a way to put their values to work, no matter what industry they're in.

4. **A strong vision for making a difference**: Elon Musk, co-founder of Paypal, CEO of Tesla Motors and SpaceX and Chairman of Solar City, talks about why he is focused on sustainable solutions, saying, "when I was in college, I decided I wanted to be involved in things that would have a significant impact on the future of humanity. And the three things I could come up with were the Internet, sustainable energy (both production and consumption), and space exploration, particularly the extension of life beyond Earth to multiple planets" (Musk, 2011). He concludes that as a leader today, there have to be things that inspire you to be proud to be a member of humanity.

5. **An inclusive style that engenders trust**: few people have taken inclusive leadership as far as Ricardo Semler, CEO of Semco, a $1 billion+ multinational company headquartered in Brazil. In his autobiography *Maverick* (Semler, 1993), he distils his business philosophy by saying, "We hire adults and then we treat them like adults." Hence, staff are given full access to all company information, including financial accounts and everyone else's salaries. Employees even set their own salaries and work schedules and Semler shares his job—there are now six co-CEOs who rotate leadership every six months (Blakeman, 2014).

6. **A willingness to innovate and be radical**: Jeffrey Swartz, CEO of Timberland, says, "Future capabilities will be very different, and will put a premium on lateral thinking and cross-functional, collaborative problem solving" (Accenture and UN Global Compact, 2010). Timberland demonstrated this ability most recently through an unexpected collaboration with tire manufacturer and distributor Omni United, to create a co-branded line of tires under the Timberland and Radar Tires brands. Timberland Tires will be the first tires ever purposely designed to be recycled into footwear outsoles after their journey on the road is complete.

7. **A long-term perspective on impacts:** Neil Carson, CEO of Johnson Matthey, believes that "companies think much longer term than governments and good companies think much longer term than bad companies" (Carson, 2010). As Dominic Barton, McKinsey's managing director, put it, sustainability leaders do not "remain trapped in value-destroying short-termism" but rather act as "a powerful force for instituting the kind of balanced, long-term capitalism that ultimately benefits everyone" (Barton and Wiseman, 2014).

Does your CEO pass the test? Perhaps that's too much pressure to put on a single individual. In fact, we all have the potential to be part of the new generation of sustainability leaders, whatever our area of practice, whatever our role and whatever our level of seniority. This is what MIT Professor Deborah Ancona calls "distributed leadership" (Ancona and Backman, 2010). For ultimately, we all share responsibility for inspiring and supporting others to follow our vision, passion and example for a better world.

2
Unlocking change through enterprise reform

Revisiting the purpose of business

Transformational leadership is a good place to start, but is that enough to change companies? Can we reform the business institution itself?

I believe we can, starting with reimagining the purpose of business. We sometimes forget that revolutionary change is more often the result of new ways of thinking about things (i.e. changes in perception) than new ways of doing things. So how might this apply this thinking to business? What are the new perspectives that are beginning to challenge the old way of thinking about and doing business? And is there a common thread or theme that runs through the heart of these new insights?

Let's begin with the basic assumptions about business that have come on trial of late. There are many, but I will focus on only three of the most important, namely profit, competition and rationality.

On the issue of profit, the old paradigm belief holds that the ultimate and sole function, goal and responsibility of business are to make a financial profit.

Although this belief has been tempered by a growing awareness of social responsibility since the 1960s, the mind-set of the vast majority of business leaders still places exclusive profit-making firmly at the apex of the business pyramid. Everything else is regarded as peripheral to this core process.

Such emphasis on short-term individual gain all too often results in the long-term wellbeing of employees, the community, society and the environment being sacrificed as pawns in a ruthless game of corporate chess.

This approach—with its tacit assumption that people are primarily motivated by conquest and material acquisition—has been a major limiting factor in managers' ability to tap the human potential of their organizations in any significant way.

The call now being sounded therefore is for what US futurist Willis Harman (1980) calls a new "central project" in business. This transformed focus could include service to society as the key goal of business. Enhanced quality of life could be its guiding principle and a strong set of ethics and values its foundation. Further, the search for meaning and creativity in the workplace, as well as holistic personal and collective learning, could become the key measures of performance within an organization.

This image may not be as far-fetched as many would suppose. UK business commentator Francis Kinsman (1990) for example, cites evidence from an SRI International study which suggests that a growing proportion of British society (more than a third) is becoming "inner directed" in nature. These are people whose behaviour is typically driven by non-materialistic factors and whose emphasis is more on the esoteric and qualitative than the material and quantitative.

An outstanding example of an inner directed personality would be the late Anita Roddick—one of the most remarkable business leaders to have experimented with a new "central project". As you probably know, she was founder and director of The Body Shop, a global cosmetics business (now part of L'Oreal).

The way Roddick (2005) talked about her beliefs and business philosophy makes it clear that a non-materialistic approach to business does not preclude success:

> The status quo says that the business of business is to make profits. We have always challenged that. For us the business of business is to keep the company alive and breathlessly excited, to protect the work force, to be a force for good in our society and then, after all that, to think of the speculators (shareholders).

So the heart of the message is not that profits be abandoned as a measure of business success, only that they cease to be the ultimate focus and assumed motive. After all, we need to breathe to live but breathing is not the grand purpose of our existence. Just so, profits need to become the means rather than the end of commercial activity.

A new paradigm belief, therefore, could be that service to society and the Earth is the core purpose, goal and responsibility of business.

In search of co-operative advantage

Another common old paradigm belief holds that competition is the law of the market and promotes effective and efficient business performance.

This belief, commonly paraphrased as "survival of the fittest", has long been upheld as the bastion of modern business. The assumption is that, not only does competition drive people and organizations to perform at their best, but that the collective effect of this competitive behaviour is one that is in the best interest of society at large. Mounting evidence, however, points to this assumption being questionable on both counts.

First, extensive work by Alfie Kohn (1993) suggests that, both in an educational and a business context, competitive behaviour undermines individual and group performance, whereas co-operation enhances it. Kohn also makes the point that competition in nature is extremely limited and always takes place within the larger context of co-operation.

Similarly, Rosabeth Moss Kanter (1989), Professor of Business Administration at Harvard Business School and respected consultant and author, believes that co-operation, not competition, is becoming the survival imperative in the marketplace of tomorrow. She talks about the old adversarial model and the ways in which she sees the new paradigm of co-operation beginning to manifest itself, saying:

> Today the strategic challenge of doing more with less leads companies to look outward as well as inward for solutions to the competitiveness dilemma ... Lean, agile, post-entrepreneurial companies can stretch in three ways. They pool their resources with others, ally to exploit an opportunity or link systems in a partnership. In short, they can become better "PAL's" with other organisations—from venture collaborators to suppliers, service contractors, customers and even unions. The adversarial mode with its paranoid world view centres on images of domination and fear of being dominated. It stands in stark contrast to the co-operation mode better suited to the challenge of the global (corporate) Olympics.

This theme of interdependence and connectedness is actually the basis for a powerful alternative theory, which can be applied not only to economics but to business as well. Pioneer in this field is MIT's Peter Senge (2006) who describes the emerging discipline of "systems thinking" and its merits as follows:

> Systems thinking is a discipline for seeing wholes. It is a framework for seeing interrelatedness rather than things, for seeing patterns of change rather than static "snapshots" ... And systems thinking is a

> sensibility—for the subtle interconnectedness that gives living systems their unique character. Today, systems thinking is needed more than ever because we are becoming overwhelmed by complexity ... All around us are examples of "systemic breakdowns"—problems that have no simple local cause ... Systems thinking is a discipline for seeing the "structures" that underlie complex situations and for discerning high from low leverage change. That is, by seeing wholes we learn how to foster health. To do so, systems thinking offers a language that begins by restructuring the way we think.

All of these insights, therefore, seem to point towards a new business paradigm involving greater co-operation. John Dalla Costa (1991) who, after first studying for the Catholic priesthood, later went on to become president and chief executive of one of Canada's most successful advertising agencies, describes this as "the model of reciprocity—giving back to nature, to our people and to our society as much as we in business extract from them".

A new business paradigm belief, therefore, could be that co-operation and reciprocity are the guiding principles by which business can create synergies within the greater living system.

Embracing the art of business

Another popular old paradigm belief holds that business is essentially a rational undertaking and should rely exclusively on the faculties of reason and analysis to support all of its processes.

This belief is a direct "hangover" from the mechanistic Newtonian era with its assumptions about objectivity and the rigid scientific method of proof. After all, it was the reductionist spirit of this period which led Frederick Taylor to his concept of "scientific management" and Max Weber's to his of "bureaucratic organization".

A critique of these managerial approaches was delivered by the now famed Robert Waterman and Tom Peters duo in *In Search of Excellence*:

> Professionalism in management is regularly equated with hard-headed rationality ... The problem with the rationalist view of organizing people (however) is that people are not very rational. To fit Taylor's old model, or today's organizational charts, man is simple designed wrong (or, of course, vice versa, according to our argument here). In fact, if our understanding of the current state of psychology is even close to correct, man is the ultimate study in conflict and paradox. (Waterman and Peters, 1985)

The successful performance of split-brain surgery seems to confirm this view as well as lend some insight. Doctors found that, not only can the two hemispheres of our brain operate independent of one another, but that they also seem to control essentially opposite functions. While the left-brain is associated with rational and intellectual engagements, the right-brain is oriented more towards intuitive and creative processes.

This theme of duality and balance is one which the ancient Chinese understood well and is represented by their Tai Chi symbol which depicts the flow of opposites within a greater whole. Contained within the circular symbol, the one extreme (*yin*) represents the feminine, passive, co-operative and flexible while the other (*yang*) symbolizes the masculine, active, competitive and rigid.

The possible implication of these ideas for business in the new paradigm is that, while in the past left-brain type thinking and actions have been emphasized and rewarded, there is great value to be gained from encouraging the counterbalance of a more right-brain orientation.

This may include greater respect for the role of intuition in decision-making, a restructuring of the workplace to encourage creativity among employees, more emphasis on co-operation as opposed to the competitive attitudes of the past, more flexibility in organizational design and a review of existing patriarchal systems and practices within business.

Hence, a new paradigm belief could be that business is first and foremost a human institution and should strive to be more holistic, reflecting a balance between symbolically masculine and feminine qualities.

I believe that questioning the assumptions and themes that drive business is an essential prerequisite for transformation. They are by no means sacred truths cast in stone but rather evolving concepts of an ongoing experiment. Anita Roddick captures the essence when she said: "What are we trying to do is to create a new business paradigm simply showing that business can have a human face and a social conscience" (Roddick, 2005).

That reminds me of the beautiful African idea of *ubuntu*, also referred to as "African humanism", which is encapsulated in the Xhosa proverb that "a person is a person through other people". How about that for an alternative belief system for business?

Shapeshifting the corporation

Many believe that changing our underlying beliefs about the purpose of business is not enough. We also need to translate this into new legal structures for the corporation. This has led to the rise of social businesses.

The notion of a social enterprise—a business that explicitly strives to create wider societal benefits, rather than focusing narrowly on shareholder returns—is not new. In the 1700s and 1800s, a charter of incorporation was only bestowed on those businesses that were socially useful—for example, water utilities or railroads.

As Joel Bakan, legal academic and author of *The Corporation* (Bakan, 2004), explained to me:

> The original notion of the corporation was that the sovereign would grant the status of corporation to a group of business people in order to acquit themselves of some responsibility to create something that was in the public good … The notion that this was simply about creating wealth for the owners of the company was alien.

The 18th and 19th centuries also saw the birth of the co-operative and credit union movements, initially in Britain, France and Germany, and later spreading across the globe. Today, according to the International Co-operative Alliance, more than a billion people are members of co-operatives worldwide, with co-operatives providing 100 million jobs (20% more than multinational enterprises).

The economic activity of the largest 300 co-operatives in the world equals that of the tenth largest national economy. In the US alone, there are more than 29,000 co-operatives, accounting for more than $3 trillion (£1.9 trillion) in assets, generating more than $500 billion in revenue and $25 billion in wages.

Despite these noble roots, and the existence of co-operatives as an institutional alternative, the modern corporation with its short-term, shareholder-driven mission has come to dominate our global economic landscape. Multinationals especially are seen by a growing tide of critics as not only failing to act in the interests of the public good, but as being agents of wholesale value destruction in communities, economies and the environment.

Bakan (2004) goes so far as to argue that today's companies are pathological in nature, in the sense that "the corporation has a legally defined mandate to relentlessly pursue—without exception—its own self-interest, regardless of the often harmful consequences it might cause to others".

Partly in reaction to the growing power and impact of big business, we have seen the rise of another countermovement over the past 40 years, focused on social and environmental entrepreneurs. Among early pioneers were the Ashoka Foundation (established in 1980), Fundes (1985) and the Social Venture Network (1987), with a new wave of momentum coming from high-profile cash injections by the Schwabb Foundation (1998) and Skoll Foundation (1999) and books such as *The Power of Unreasonable People* (Elkington and Hartigan, 2008).

Within the big corporates over the same period, corporate social responsibility and sustainable development programmes have gained ground, moving through defensive, charitable, promotional and strategic stages, as I have described elsewhere. However, in the face of growing pressure to prioritize their fiduciary duty towards shareholders, these CSR and "triple bottom line" efforts have been widely criticized as little more than window-dressing and corporate spin, and largely ineffective in tackling our most pressing social and environmental crises.

The solution, say a new breed of business activists, is to change the legal obligations of corporations, in order to resolve the growing conflict between their fiduciary duty to shareholders and their ethical accountability to other stakeholder groups. Encouragingly, the regulators seem to be listening, as evidenced by a spate of new legal corporate structures being promulgated around the world which are specifically designed to recognize and support social enterprises.

The UK's "community interest company" (CIC) structure was among the first. In terms of the legislation, a CIC is a limited liability company in all respects, but has an explicitly stated social purpose and is committed to reinvest its profits and assets in furthering those social aims. According to the CIC regulator, there are around 10,000 community interest companies registered.

The US followed in 2007 with the introduction of the "benefit corporation", or B Corp, as proposed by B Lab, a not-for-profit organization, which initiated a certification system for companies interested in distinguishing themselves as socially responsible. Unlike other certification schemes such as the ISO 14001 or SA 8000, the B Corp system has gone on to be legally recognized as a new institutional form in 27 US states, with 14 more states working on legislation. As of March 2015, there were more than 1,212 B Corps covering 121 industries in 38 countries.

According to Dermot Hikisch (2013), B Lab's head of community development:

> B Corps are now found in virtually every industry, with some like
> Agora Partnerships being set-up as social enterprises from day one,
> while others like Ben & Jerry's come from traditional industries and
> have found a way to do things better.

In 2012, Ben & Jerry's became the first wholly owned subsidiary in the world to be certified as a B Corp. Chief executive Jostein Solheim noted: "When Ben & Jerry's was acquired [by Unilever], many folks thought it would be a challenge for the company to keep its values." Now, B Corp certification is "the chance to affirm that we remain true to our mission and look to accelerate our social impact" (Confino, 2012).

Another milestone was passed in December 2014 when Brazil's top cosmetics, fragrance and toiletries maker, Natura, became the largest—and first publicly traded—company to attain B Corp certification.

In the US, there is also the option to register as a low-profit limited liability company (L3C), now legally recognized in nine states. It allows similar benefits to other social enterprise forms, but is specifically designed to qualify as a programme-related investment (PRI), which is one of the ways foundations can satisfy their obligation under the Tax Reform Act of 1969 to distribute at least 5% of their assets every year for charitable purposes.

A further and more recent variation is the flexible purpose corporation (FPC) in California. It is intended to allow shareholders to determine for themselves their own preferred mix of social and economic corporate objectives. According to Hikisch (2013): "It may help a larger company's executives have safe harbour for following a single social mission, but there's no requirement to consider all stakeholders and no requirement as to the scale of the impact."

Hikisch thinks FPCs are unlikely to be widely adopted by social enterprises because they aren't obligated to pursue generalized public benefit nor required to measure their performance against any third-party standard.

There are a number of major benefits in these new legal forms of incorporation for social enterprises and responsible companies. First, it may improve access to capital or funding, even though there are no direct tax benefits. For example, arts and crafts e-commerce site Etsy used its B Corp certification to help secure funding of $40 million. According to chief executive Chad Dickerson, it "gave us a framework to measure Etsy's success against rigorous values and responsible practices as we scale as a company".

Second, there is the possibility of brand differentiation, with its associated reputational kudos. Third, and perhaps most important, it can give directors a shareholder mandate to pursuit broader stakeholder value beyond financial returns. It may also be a weapon in the so-called "war for talent"—a way to signal to potential and existing employees that the business has a more noble purpose than moneymaking.

Ultimately, if corporations are successful in shapeshifting—right down to their legally constituted core—perhaps business will even be able to discard the mantle of the psychopath and be accepted back into the community as a rehabilitated corporate citizen.

Family-friendly enterprises

Changing the mission and legal structure is one thing. But changing the corporate culture to be more values-based may be even more critical. Consider that only 21% of employees globally (14% in the UK) are fully engaged in their work, according to a Towers Watson global workforce survey. In the UK, one in four (24%) are not satisfied with their job and nearly one in three (30%) do not feel engaged by their employer.

This is no trivial matter. Gallup estimates the cost of employee disengagement to the UK economy to be somewhere between £59.4 billion and £64.7 billion. Part of this cost is sickness-related absence; engaged employees in the UK take an average of 2.7 sick days per year, compared with 6.2 for those who could be described as disengaged.

The Centre for Mental Health estimates that employers loose around £8.4 billion a year this way. However, nearly double this amount (£15.1 billion a year) is due to productivity loss from people not feeling well in the workplace, so-called presenteeism.

Turn the trend around, however, and there are big upsides to having an engaged workforce. Research by the Corporate Leadership Council (2004) suggests that engaged employees are 87% less likely to leave their organization. According to the IES/Work Foundation, if companies increased investment in workplace engagement by 10%, they would increase profits by £1,500 per employee per year. That is because engaged employees generate 43% more revenue than disengaged ones and highly engaged organizations have the potential to reduce staff turnover by 87% and improve performance by 20%.

Given these statistics, it is hardly surprising that issues of wellbeing in the workplace are on the rise. In the UK, Business in the Community (BITC) promotes this agenda through their Workwell campaign, while globally the

Great Place to Work Institute partners with more than 5,500 organizations with around ten million employees to conduct the largest annual set of workplace culture studies in the world.

According to their research, employees believe they work for great organizations when they trust the people they work for, have pride in what they do and enjoy the people they work with.

Great Place to Work's annual surveys and awards give kudos and some PR-driven reputational payback for companies that are investing in workplace wellbeing. For example, Microsoft has consistently been in the top ten best multinationals to work for globally, and has led the ranking for Europe for the past four years.

"For us that means greater creativity, greater productivity and, ultimately, continued success as a market leader," says Michel Van der Bel, managing director for Microsoft UK says. Google topped the global as well as the Asia leader board in 2014. Importantly, Great Place to Work also recognizes large national companies and small and medium-sized enterprises.

Awards are one way to recognize best practice. Another is certification of management systems, which tends to encourage greater embedding of the values in the organization. One place where this is happening is Slovenia, where the Ministry of Labour, Family and Social Affairs, in partnership with auditing firm The Ekvilib Institute, has run a family-friendly enterprise certification scheme since 2007. To date, more than 130 companies, employing around 50,000 workers (7% of Slovenian workforce) have been certified. The certification scheme is based on the European family audit system developed by the German organization Berufundfamilie and currently used in Germany, Austria, Hungary and Italy.

In Slovenia, the certification focuses on employer practices that support work–life balance, especially creating a work environment that supports women with young children that do not want to make a trade-off between career aspirations and family commitments.

For example, employees with children are given flexible working hours and additional leave days. Various stress relief programmes are also offered, and a special team is established to introduce better methods of work which co-ordinate professional and family life, including services such as counselling, childcare, babysitters, vacation offers and spaces for children in the company.

Some leading role models in these practices in Slovenia include Dejan Turk, the relatively young chief executive of Si.mobil, the country's second biggest mobile operator, as well as Matjaz Cadez, founder and former chief executive of the IT company Halcom, and the Ursic brothers, who own a small manufacturing company called IMAS.

But family-friendly enterprise goes beyond the good reputations of a few. The results across all the Slovenian certified companies are impressive. Research shows that these businesses benefit commercially in a number of other ways. In particular they achieve a reduction in staff turnover and sick leave, along with higher employee productivity, motivation, satisfaction and commitment.

Apart from these quantifiable business case benefits, family-friendly enterprise is also about a shift in leadership perceptions and organizational culture. According to Ales Kranjc Kuslan (2013), director of Ekvilib Institute, in their certified companies, "top management start to think of employees as partners and a long term investment, rather than just another cost".

Petra Hartman (2013), project officer at Ekvilib Institute, believes this is even more critical in a recessionary environment. "In times of economic crisis, companies will have to be creative in rewarding their employees in non-financial ways."

And what better way than by creating a work environment that supports not only you and your job, but also your family and your quality of life.

On the road to a cycling revolution?

One great way to support families and quality of life is for companies to promote cycling among their employees. It's not only good for personal health, but also good for the planet, and especially good for congested cities.

In March 2013, London mayor Boris Johnson—already feted for his pay-as-you-go "Boris bikes" introduced in 2010—announced plans for the longest bike route in any European city. This is part of a £1 billion bid to double the number of Londoners who cycle over the next decade.

This is certainly welcome news for a city that hopes to reduce its carbon footprint by 60% by 2025. Currently, the average Londoner emits 9.6 tonnes of CO_2 per year, which is lower than New York (10.5 tonnes), but almost three times Stockholm (3.6 tonnes), despite Sweden having a far colder climate. Cycling is one obvious way to make a dent on our carbon footprint in the west. But are we convinced?

According to the CTC, the UK national cycling association, a person making the average daily commute of four miles each way would save half a tonne of carbon dioxide per year if they switched from driving to cycling per year. If the UK doubled cycle use by switching from cars, this would reduce Britain's total greenhouse emissions by 0.6 million tonnes, almost as much as switching all London-to-Scotland air travel to rail.

There are obvious health benefits from cycling as well. One classic study found that, while people are killed each year in the UK while cycling (in 2012, 122 cyclists died), many others die prematurely because of lack of exercise. The study estimated that regular cycling provides a net benefit to personal health that outweighs its risk of injury by a factor of 20 to one. If anything, the situation is more extreme today, with estimates that, if things don't change, 60% of men and 50% of women will be obese by 2050.

The UK charity, PleaseCycle (2012) says the benefits of cycling are demonstrated with some handy statistics. It reports that 79% of employees wish their employers had a more positive outlook on cycling and a 20% increase in cycling by 2015 could save £87 million in reduced absenteeism. The charity also claims there is up to 12.5% difference in productivity between exercising and non-exercising employees and regular cycling can reduce a person's all-cause mortality rate by up to 36%.

Even the economic benefits are compelling. The specialist economic consultancy SQW showed that an increase in cycling by 20% would release cumulative saving of £500 million by 2015. A 50% increase on current cycling rates would unlock more than £1.3 billion, by reducing the costs of congestion, pollution and healthcare.

So why aren't more of us cycling? Surely it's not that we're all just lazy? This is where I believe we can learn some lessons from other countries—the Netherlands in particular. The Dutch have turned cycling into a national pastime and the bicycle into a cultural icon: wherever you go in the country, there are swift-flowing rivers of cyclists.

The population of the Netherlands is under 17 million—roughly twice that of New York or London—yet they make more cycle journeys than 313 million Americans, 63 million British and 22 million Australians put together, and they do so with greater safety than cyclists in any of those countries. Londoners only make around 2% of journeys by bike, and New Yorkers even fewer, at only around 0.6% of commutes. Meanwhile, in the Netherlands on an average working day, five million people make an average of 14 million cycle journeys.

So why, in an age desperate for more sustainable transport solutions, has the Netherlands succeeded so spectacularly where others have tried and failed? There seem to be a few obvious reasons. First, the country is relatively flat. Second, it is fairly small, so vehicle space is at a premium. Third, the government has invested heavily in supporting infrastructure such as bike lanes and storage facilities. And fourth, cycling is complemented by a well-developed public transport system of trains, buses and trams.

There is also the very important issue of safety—both perceived and actual. The accident statistics show that the Netherlands is the safest place in the world to cycle. There is obviously a safety in numbers effect, and good infrastructure design is vital. But there are also legal sanctions. For example, there is an interesting law in the Netherlands, which makes car drivers financially responsible in the event of a crash with bikers. Of course, there is a cultural effect as well. Since everyone cycles regularly, there is a prevailing empathy and safety awareness on the roads.

Back in the UK, the signs are encouraging. According to the charity Sustrans (2012), in 2011 there was a 15% increase in trips on the National Cycle Network, with 484 million journeys made by 3.3 million individuals. The estimated health benefits of all this activity were worth £442 million.

There are also some neat innovations. For example, PleaseCycle has an app that helps companies to engage their employees and help them to track their bike miles and associated benefits such as carbon savings. Aegis Media used the app for its three main London offices during the 2012 Olympics. By signing up just 5% of its workforce, more than 800 journeys were logged and 5,000 bike miles were clocked up over a four-week period. The 1.5 tonnes of CO_2 saved was equivalent to flying from London to Paris six times.

Admittedly, it's not quite a revolution yet, but there are at least signs of an uprising—slowly but surely, more and more of us are rising from the sofa, out of the car seat and onto our bikes.

Small is beautiful and sustainable

The good thing about family-friendly workplaces and promoting bike riding is that any company can do it—large or small. It is true that small and medium-sized enterprises (SMEs) face many barriers in adopting sustainable business practices, but with a little creativity, collaboration and help from government, things could change.

Take Mexico, for example, where small and medium-sized enterprises account for more than 99% of the four million businesses in the country, as well as generating 52% of GDP and providing 72% of employment. The government's business accelerator programme supports these SMEs by funding institutions that can help the sector grow by improving competitiveness, business opportunities and market scalability.

One such business accelerator is the IDEARSE Center at Anahuac University in Mexico City. The centre's business model for SME acceleration is built around corporate social responsibility (CSR), incorporating environmental impacts, human rights, self-regulation, social impacts and community involvement and stakeholder engagement.

More remarkable still is that, by working with the supply chains of big brands such as Sony, Coca-Cola and Cemex and having trained more than 150 SMEs since 2007, the SMEs achieved sales growth of between 5% and 37% and jobs growth of between 5% and 19%. At the same time SME performance across all six CSR areas has improved between 23% and 46%. These numbers debunk several popular myths, most notably that CSR is not relevant, too expensive or not incentivized for SMEs. Let's look more closely at these myths.

Is CSR relevant for SMEs? The issue of relevance largely hinges on whether you adopt a very literal and narrow interpretation of CSR. Laura Spence (2012), director of the Royal Holloway, University of London's Centre for Research into Sustainability, says that the terminology of CSR is both inaccurate (as small firms are unlikely to be corporations) and off-putting jargon for SMEs.

"Also since CSR practice is often associated with reporting, SMEs don't stand a chance. They are unlikely to have external financial reports, let alone the time resources or need to produce a glossy CSR report," says Spence (2012).

So first, we need to get the labels and definitions right. The IDEARSE centre, for example, describes CSR as "a permanent and continuous commitment, voluntarily adopted by the business, to respond to the economic, social and environmental impacts of its activities, and to guarantee the sustainable and human development to all its stakeholders". No doubt, it helps that CSR in Spanish (*responsabilidad social empresarial* or RSE) translates more accurately as socially responsible "enterprise".

The second issue—whether CSR is too costly—is a real concern, but once again, it depends what we mean by CSR. Work by CSR academics Dirk Matten and Jeremy Moon distinguish between explicit and implicit CSR (Matten and Moon, 2008). Explicit CSR refers to many of the formalized practices we associate with large corporates, such as CSR codes, standards, managers, systems, reports and audits. These are resource intensive and mostly not feasible for SMEs.

Implicit CSR, on the other hand, includes informal ethical practices that are not dependent on size or financial muscle. "If you talk about the content of a socially responsible business—integrity, reputation, caring for employees, building relationships, community engagement—that is often simply an everyday part of SME life," Spence says. Many SMEs, thus, are practising social responsibility without even knowing it or needing to give it a CSR label.

Besides these implicit CSR practices, Itzel Lopez (2012) of the IDEARSE centre says that CSR is often crucial for SMEs because it can be "a requirement imposed, not by the law, but by the market itself".

She is referring to the growing practice of large companies in demanding ethical standards of their suppliers. Nike's supplier code of conduct and Walmart's supplier sustainability assessment are two cases that increasingly illustrate the rule rather than the exception.

There is also a middle ground between too costly (explicit CSR) and business critical (supply chain compliance). As with CSR practised by multinationals, SMEs can often find a business case in cost savings from eco-efficiency, especially from reductions in waste, water and energy. Furthermore, Lopez believes that "CSR strategies can lend prestige and boost consumer confidence. They can also increase productivity by motivating employees and encourage loyalty."

We should also not totally discount formalized CSR practices among SMEs. One of the things I observed when visiting the sugar plantations of Guatemala was that they had formed a co-operative of farms in order to tackle CSR. Individually, they were too small to justify a sustainable business programme, but collectively, it made sense. This is one of the ways that SMEs can address CSR, through pooling their resources and collaborating.

On the issue of incentives, as most SMEs are owner-managed, the values of the director play a crucial role. My experience has been that most SME owners live in their communities and that responsibility often comes naturally to them. After all, they usually have to personally interact with their customers every day. The exceptions tend to be when SMEs are entirely set up for export and their employees are not also their customers. This not only creates worker dependence, but also low accountability for impacts on the community and environment.

Besides the moral orientation of SME owners, governments can also help to create incentives for CSR adoption. It is no surprise that the IDEARSE centre was selected as one of the business accelerators in Mexico, since the government developed a national CSR standard in 2004 and has subsequently adopted ISO 26000 on social responsibility as a best practice guideline. Local support is also important. For instance, some years back I observed a local government agency in Scotland that had established a dedicated unit to offer free sustainable business advisory services to SMEs.

There is no denying that SMEs face many barriers—from alienating definitions and weak incentives to prohibitive costs and heavy-handed supply chain audits. But at least perceptions are changing and the evidence of benefits is mounting. There are also helpful tools, such as the Primer on Business Sustainability for SMEs and ACCA's report on Environmental Aspects of Sustainability: SMEs and the Role of the Accountant.

I look forward to the day when pioneering British economist E.F. Schumacher's small is beautiful idiom applies as much to sustainable business as to economic activity. If Mexico's example is anything to go by, that day may come sooner than we expect.

Tracking the footprints of trade

One of the strongest drivers for sustainability among SMEs, just mentioned, are ethical standards being imposed on the supply chain. So let's look at an example of how this is playing out in practice, namely the Kenyan floriculture market.

There are flowers to fit every occasion. But if you are celebrating World Water Week (26–31 August), you might want to think twice. A single rose—grown in Kenya, as many of the world's cut flowers are—takes around 10 litres of water to produce, with the so-called water footprint, or virtual water export, of Kenya's floriculture industry having more than doubled over the past 15 years, mostly to supply the Netherlands (69%), the UK (18%) and Germany (7%).

This notion of virtual water—the water embedded in the things that we trade—is gaining visibility as awareness of our global water crisis increases. I remember first getting to grips with the idea a few years ago when I interviewed Fred Pearce, author of *When the Rivers Run Dry* (Pearce, 2006), for the University of Cambridge *Top 50 Sustainability Books* (Visser and CPSL, 2009) project. According to his calculations, to get us through the day, it takes about a hundred times our own weight in water.

Of course, water footprints are not the only impacts we find in our global supply chains. There are issues of labour rights, climate change, transparent governance, biodiversity loss and economic development, to mention but a few. The challenge is to manage and minimize the negative impacts. This is where I believe the example of Kenya's cut-flower industry can help us to tease out some hard-won lessons, starting with the story behind the Horticultural Ethical Business Initiative (HEBI).

The seeds of the HEBI process were sown in November 1999 when local civil society organizations mounted a successful campaign against workers' rights violations in Cirio Delmonte, one of Kenya's largest pineapple growers. The success of this campaign raised concerns in the flower industry, prompting stakeholders to develop the Kenya Standard on Social Accountability and a Voluntary Private Initiative to oversee its implementation.

However, the real impetus for HEBI came from the pressure exerted by transnational alliances of NGOs and consumer groups. The Kenya Women Workers Organisation (KEWWO) was funded by the UK-based Women Working Worldwide (WWW) to gather evidence of the Ethical Trade Initiative Base Code violations. Their report catalogued various unacceptable conditions, from pesticide poisoning to sexual harassment and rape, and spurred a campaign dubbed Produce Safely or Quit. At the same time, the Kenya Human Rights Commission issued a three-month ultimatum to flower producers to improve working conditions, failing which they would go international in their campaign.

When the Ethical Trading Initiative (ETI) was alerted to these serious labour rights violations in 2002, several of their corporate and NGO members visited Kenyan flower producers. In fear of losing their most significant market, Kenyan stakeholders came together for the first time to lay the groundwork for the formation of HEBI. What I find particular interesting is that the Horticultural Ethical Business Initiative (HEBI) did not arise from a vacuum of voluntary codes. On the contrary, there were already seven different international ethical codes being applied. However, they seemed to lack effectiveness and credibility.

What made HEBI both necessary and different was the need to involve all stakeholders. As academic experts Catherine Dolan and Maggie Opondo put it:

> In contrast to the Fresh Produce Exporters Association of Kenya, the Kenya Flower Council and the Voluntary Private Initiative, which were locally initiated attempts to protect the image of the industry in overseas markets, HEBI was a product of direct Northern involvement.

> While ETI and WWW only performed a facilitative role in the process,
> they were nonetheless pivotal to the establishment of a locally owned
> multi-stakeholder process. (Dolan and Opondo, 2005)

Today, according to ETI, there is still a lot of work to be done and plenty to criticize, but changes to the audit process and the purchasing practices of ETI members have led to a number improvements for workers in Kenya. For example, there are now more permanent contracts, establishment of worker welfare and gender committees, better provision of protective equipment, stricter pesticide controls and extensive improvements in housing. Furthermore, more women now have access to day-care facilities and there is general acceptance that pregnant women should have light duties.

Most encouragingly, Kenya's convoluted and painful journey to creating their multi-stakeholder sector code has set a benchmark for other standards, such as the Roundtable on Sustainable Palm Oil (RSPO), to learn from and emulate. It has also inspired complementary programmes such as The Floriculture Sustainability Initiative, part of the Dutch Sustainable Trade Initiative (IDH), which aims to accelerate and upscale sustainable trade by building impact oriented coalitions of front running multinationals, civil society organizations, governments and other stakeholders.

So, yes, flowers do have footprints. But perhaps, if we learn from Kenya's experiences, we can lighten the tread and ensure those footprints are heading in a more sustainable direction.

Women as sustainable business advocates

Another interesting feature of the Kenya flowers case was the critical role that women played in improving standards. This is something I also noticed a few years ago, on one of my visits to China, when I was invited to speak to a group in Shanghai called Women in Sustainability Action (Wisa). The organization was set up by a former academic colleague, Jacylyn Shi, as a global network of professional women working in sustainability. This got me thinking about the relationship between women and sustainability—and especially how this dynamic is playing out in China.

According to Professor Kellie McElhaney, founder of the Centre for Responsible Business at University of California, Berkeley's Haas School of Business, companies that empower women are more likely to be companies that act sustainably.

A research paper written by McElhaney and Sanaz Mobasseri found that businesses with more women on their board of directors bring a string of sustainability benefits (McElhaney and Mobasseri, 2012). Specifically, these companies are more likely to: manage and improve their energy efficiency; measure and reduce their carbon emissions; reduce their packaging impacts; invest in renewable power; improve access to healthcare in developing countries; have strong partnerships with local communities; offer products with nutritional or health benefits; proactively manage human capital development; offer transparent financial products; have anticorruption policies and programmes; have a high level of disclosure and transparency; and avoid controversies such as accounting fraud, price fixing, criminal behaviour among top executives, controversial customer practices and insider trading.

But why is this? It's a topic for hot debate and there are probably as many opinions as there are commentators. Do men have inherently unsustainable ways of acting in the world? Does testosterone fuel the exploitation of our planet and its people? Are women our best hope for creating a sustainable future?

Elle Carberry (2012), co-founder and managing director of the China Greentech Initiative, believes that women may be drawn to sustainability because of its social angle. "From all my 20 years in business, I have met more women in this area than in others, be it in China or the United States." She adds: "It does strike me that women come to this with a view about society and business."

For one Chinese woman in particular, this "view about society and business" turned her into the wealthiest self-made woman in the world. Zhang Yin, also known by her Cantonese name Cheung Yan, is the founder and director of Nine Dragons Paper, a recycling company that buys scrap paper from the US, imports it into China, and turns it mainly into cardboard for use in boxes to export Chinese goods.

In 2006, she topped the list of the richest people in China and by 2010 her $4.6 billion (£2.9 billion) fortune placed her ahead of the likes of Oprah Winfrey and J.K. Rowling. She has said that she built her entire business empire on some simple advice that she received in Hong Kong in 1985: "Waste paper is like a forest—paper recycles itself, generation after generation."

And she is not alone in her vision. Peggy Liu, co-founder of the Joint US–China Collaboration on Clean Energy (Juccce), is working to create a China Dream concept to divert China away from a mass consumerist path and is targeting high-level officials to spread her message and give foreign companies and experts access to China's decision-makers.

Carberry (2012) believes that "the markets associated with China going green might be some of the biggest markets ever". She approached the head of General Electric (GE) in China in 2008 and asked if he would support a knowledge sharing platform and network to help accelerate the scaling of clean technology.

"He jumped at the idea immediately," she recalls. "And when I asked him why he was so keen, he said, 'in China the opportunity is too big, the problem is too urgent and China is too complex. We can't do it alone. We all—GE, Dow, Bayer and others—see a piece of it, but none of us see how the whole thing comes together'." And so the China Greentech Initiative was born.

Today, the platform pulls together information on cleantech, checks and analyses that data and brings together a network of interested companies, policy-makers and organizations to identify opportunities. It certainly seems to be working. According to the Ernst & Young ranking of country attractiveness for renewable energy investments, China leads the world, ahead of the US, UK, Japan and Germany (EY, 2014).

Yin and Carberry are just two of many such pioneering women taking on sustainable business in China. Others, to name but a few, include Jin JiaMan, director of the Global Environmental Institute, Chen Zhili, chair of the China Women's Federation, Li Chun Mei, founder and general manager of Wealth Environment Engineering Co, and Anne Myong, chief operating officer of Walmart, who realized the lack of leadership on CSR and is now devising a clearer strategy.

This represents progress, albeit not enough. Kaying Lau, country director for the Global Reporting Initiative in China, says despite these role models, millions of women are still underrepresented. But with more high-profile role models, the hope is that more will be empowered to join the sustainability revolution.

Where next for the circular economy?

What Zhang Yin's paper recycling company and Elle Carberry's China Greentech Initiative show is the circular economy—where closed-loop production brings us closer to the goal of zero waste—is a real business opportunity. According to Hunter Lovins, co-author of *Natural Capitalism*

(Hawken *et al.*, 1999), our global economy is so inefficient that less than 1% of all the resources we extract are actually used in products and are still there six months after sale.

Not only is this unbelievably inefficient, it is also profoundly unsustainable. As Richard Heinberg says in his book, *Peak Everything* (2007), "The 21st century ushered in an era of declines", from global oil, natural gas, and coal extraction to yearly grain harvests, climate stability, population, fresh water and minerals such as copper and platinum.

The idea of a circular economy is not new. In the 1960s, US economist Kenneth Boulding (1966) called for a shift away from a "cowboy economy", where endless frontiers imply no limits on resource consumption or waste disposal, to "spaceship economy", where everything is engineered to be constantly recycled. Mariska van Dalen (2012), a circular economy expert at the consultancy and engineering firm Tebodin, captures the essence of the concept as: "Waste is food, use solar income and celebrate diversity."

One of the most prominent advocates for the circular economy is Michael Braungart, co-author of *Cradle to Cradle* (Braungart and McDonough, 2008). Today, Braungart holds an Academic Chair in Cradle to Cradle Innovation and Quality at Rotterdam School of Management, Erasmus University (RSM) in the Netherlands, where Braungart has found his intellectual home.

When I interviewed Braungart for *The Top 50 Sustainability Books* (Visser and CPSL, 2009) a few years ago, I found out that he regards the Netherlands as most likely to become the first circular economy. "The Dutch never romanticised nature, so it's different to the United Kingdom or Germany," he said. "There's no 'mother nature', because with the next tide they would just swim away. It was always a culture of partnership with nature, learning from nature, and that's what we need. We can learn endlessly from nature, but it's not about romanticising nature."

The Netherlands also have a culture of support, whereas the Americans, Germans, British and Swedish have a culture of control, Braungart said. "They assume human beings are bad anyway and we need to control them to be less bad. But the Dutch culture is a culture of support, because if you don't support your neighbour, you will drown (because your neighbour couldn't take care of your dyke). Even if you don't like your neighbour, you need to support your neighbour. So Cradle to Cradle is a culture of support."

I was interested to find out whether experts working on the circular economy in the Netherlands also shared Braungart's confidence. Krispijn Beek, who worked at the Ministry of Economic Affairs, Innovation and Agriculture on sustainable business policy, said "Cradle to Cradle was a big hit in the

Netherlands, including government". Apparently, the trend really took off after a 2006 television documentary, *Afval = Voedsel* (Waste = Food).

However, at a later point the idea stalled—at least in government. Beek claims that "one of the showstoppers was the commercial certification process, which made it impossible to use Cradle to Cradle in public procurement".

Michel Schuurman (2012), a director at MVO Nederland, agrees that "the concept gained a lot of attention some years ago but has faded a bit in recent times". He believes the reason, at least partially, is that "businesses are in the process of experimenting with it and are not yet ready to communicate publically". Another reason is what he calls "the closed system of Cradle to Cradle"—"its monopoly, lack of transparency and (expensive) certification has been a reason for some to follow the principles but not the scheme".

Beek (2012) expresses a similar frustration.

> The Dutch government had a chance to get Cradle to Cradle thinking into the REACH regulatory framework [but] this momentum was lost because the owners of Cradle to Cradle stayed vague about their objectives against REACH and which changes would be required [to] fit into the Cradle to Cradle framework.

The private sector has seen more progress. In fact, Beek believes that a critical factor for its success here is that design of the circular economy uses a business perspective, while similar earlier concepts were too driven by nonprofits or government policy. Beek (2012) is now CSR manager at Strukton, one of the top ten construction companies in the Netherlands. "We are working on a process called 'concrete-to-concrete aggregates' (C2CA)," he says. "With international partners (universities and companies), we are recycling not only concrete but also concrete aggregates."

This is only one of many circular economy initiatives and leading corporate examples in the Netherlands. Others I have come across include Aveda, Auping, Philips and Interface FLOR. Some local municipalities and regions have also taken a lead, such as Venlo, which hosts a Cradle to Cradle expo lab and Paviljon at the annual Floriade flower exhibition.

As far as spreading these best practices goes, Schuurman (2012) observes that, so far, the circular economy has been "driven by visionary and bold leaders" and "the increasing need and desire to have closer relationships along the value chain". Van Dalen (2012) stresses that scaling up the circular economy requires it to be translated into concrete measures and clearly demonstrated as a way to meet multi-stakeholder sustainability targets.

Besides these drivers, it is also important to stimulate public debate. According to Beek, this includes ideas such as upcycling, the process of converting waste materials or useless products into new materials or products of better quality or for better environmental value, and service-lease concepts such as Turn Too, Rendemint, or Philips, where you can now lease lumen (units of luminous flux) for your office instead of buying LED lights.

Finally, we should not forget that, beyond being a solution to our global environmental crisis, the circular economy is also a business opportunity. A recent study commissioned by the Ellen MacArthur Foundation concluded that there is an annual net material cost saving opportunity of up to $380 billion (£237 billion) in a transition scenario and of up to $630 billion (£393 billion) in an advanced scenario, and that is only based on a subset of EU manufacturing sectors. "It's not about using less and less," the Foundation concludes. "It's about finding a cycle that works."

3
Unlocking change through technology innovation

How to use technology to make our planet more sustainable, not less

The drive for a circular economy means that investment is booming in clean and green technologies. But can they be implemented quickly enough to meet current challenges?

The controversial demographer Paul Ehrlich distilled the essence of his somewhat apocalyptic 1968 book, *The Population Bomb* (Ehrlich, 1968), into a simple equation: impact (I) = population (P) x affluence (A) x technology (T). Twenty years later, Ray Anderson, the sustainability pioneer and then-CEO of Interface, asked the question: what if it were possible to move T to the denominator, so that technology reduces, rather than increases, impact on the environment and society?

Anderson's challenge is the Apollo mission of the 21st century—a near impossible project that, if achieved, will inspire generations to come. The only difference is that achieving a sustainable technology revolution—let's call it Mission SusTech—is playing for much higher stakes than J.F. Kennedy's space race. Failure *is* an option and it's called "overshoot and collapse".

The good news is that Mission SusTech is well under way. This chapter will spotlight trends, breakthroughs, cases and lessons on the development and transfer of sustainable technologies around the world. But be warned: it won't focus on the latest touted miracle technologies but on the challenges of sharing, implementing and bringing to scale existing sustainable technologies.

What are the trends? Not only is technological innovation booming, but it is rapidly shifting towards sustainable solutions. For example, many of the World Economic Forum's top ten most promising technologies have a clear environmental and social focus, such as energy-efficient water purification, enhanced nutrition to drive health at the molecular level, carbon dioxide (CO_2) conversion, precise drug delivery through nanoscale engineering, organic electronics and photovoltaics.

The 2012 Global Green R&D report found that private investments in clean technology and green economic and commercial solutions reached $3.6 trillion for the period 2007–12 (Nash, 2012). This included more than $2 trillion in renewable energy, $700 billion in green construction, $241 billion in green R&D, $238 billion in the smart grid and $231 billion in energy efficiency.

For specific clean energy technologies—including wind, solar and biofuels—the market size was estimated at $248 billion in 2013 and is projected to grow to $398 billion by 2023, according to the 2014 Clean Energy Trends report (Clean Edge, 2014). Biofuels remain the largest market ($98 billion), followed by solar ($91 billion) and wind ($58 billion). In what Clean Edge (2014) hails as a tipping point, in 2013 the world installed more new solar photovoltaic generating capacity (36.5 gigawatts) than wind power (35.5 gigawatts).

This rapid growth is being fuelled by significant investment in research and development and breakthroughs in sustainable technologies, as indicated by a spike in patent applications.

According to the World Intellectual Property Organization (WIPO), more patents have been filed in the last five years than in the previous 30 across key climate change mitigation technologies, or CCMTs (biofuels, solar thermal, solar photovoltaics and wind energy). While the average global rate of patent filing grew by 6% between 2006 and 2011, these CCMTs have experienced a combined growth rate of 24% over the same period.

Contrary to what some may think, emerging markets cannot automatically be assumed to lag on sustainable technological innovation. China and the Republic of Korea have filed the most patents in recent years across all four CCMT technology areas, while in solar PV, the top 20 technology owners are based in Asia.

What does the future hold? The sustainable technology innovation wave is only just building. Research by McKinsey (2011) shows that improvements in resource productivity in energy, land, water and materials—based on better deployment of current innovative technologies—could meet up to 30% of total 2030 demand, with 70% to 85% of these opportunities occurring in developing countries. Capturing the total resource productivity opportunity could save $2.9 trillion in 2030.

We are living through the birth of what David King, director of the Smith School of Enterprise and the Environment at Oxford University, calls "another renaissance" in the industrial revolution: "Human ingenuity is the answer", says King. "We created the science and engineering technological revolution on which all our wellbeing is based. That same keen intelligence can point to the solutions to the hangover challenges and this requires nothing less than another renaissance" (World Economic Forum, 2012).

Tackling the food waste challenge with technology

The challenges of the 21st century will stretch our collective capacity for innovation like never before.

Take food security. Our mission, should we choose to accept it, is first to find 175–220 million hectares of additional cropland by 2030; second, to increase total food production by about 70% by 2050, mostly through improving crop yields; and third, to achieve all this without damaging the land, poisoning ourselves or impairing the health of our finite and already fragile ecosystems.

The Food and Agriculture Organization (FAO) estimates that meeting this challenge will require investment in developing countries' agriculture of $9.2 trillion (£5.4 trillion) over the next 44 years—about $210 billion (£123 billion) a year—from both private and public sources (Salman *et al.*, 2010). Just under half of this amount will need to go into primary agriculture, and the rest into food processing, transportation, storage and other downstream activities. A priority will be finding ways to close the gaps between crop yields in developed and developing countries, which for wheat, rice and maize respectively are around 40%, 75% and 30–200% less in developing countries—all while using fewer resources and less harmful substances.

This challenge is hard enough, but we also have to tackle the problem of 1.3 billion tonnes of food wasted every year—roughly a third of all food produced for human consumption. Fortunately, this is an area where technology can play a strong role, and where the economic, human and environmental benefits are compelling. An assessment of resource productivity opportunities between now and 2030 suggests that reducing food waste could return $252 billion (£148 billion) in savings, the third largest of all resource efficiency opportunities identified by a McKinsey study.

Although food waste is highest in Europe and North America, it is also a problem in developing regions such as sub-Saharan Africa and South and South-East Asia. According to the FAO, the total value of lost food is $4 billion per year in Africa and $4.5 billion a year in India, with up to 50% of fruit and vegetables ending up as waste. In developing countries such as China and Vietnam, most food is lost through poor handling, storage and spoilage in distribution. It is estimated that 45% of rice in China and 80% in Vietnam never make it to market for these reasons.

One of the most effective ways to reduce food waste is to improve packaging, for example by using Modified Atmosphere Packaging (MAP)—a technology that substitutes the atmosphere inside a package with a protective gas mix, typically a combination of oxygen, carbon dioxide and nitrogen—to extend freshness.

This is a well-proven solution that calls for technology transfer rather than invention, which has been the approach of the Sustainable Product Innovation Project in Vietnam. Through the project, MAP has been applied to over 1,000 small-scale farmers, resulting in reductions in postharvest food waste from 30–40% to 15–20%.

Another simple packaging solution being promoted in developing countries is the International Rice Research Institute Super Bag. When properly sealed, the bag cuts oxygen levels from 21% to 5%, reducing live insects to fewer than one insect per kg of grain—often within ten days of sealing. This extends the germination life of seeds from six to 12 months and controls insect grain pests without using chemicals.

Besides improved packaging, a second way to reduce food loss and waste is through improved storage and transportation. A new report on creating a sustainable "cold chain" in the developing world estimates that about 25–50% of food wastage could be eliminated with better, more climate friendly refrigeration. For example, Unilever has committed to using hydrocarbon (HC) refrigerants, which saved 40,000 tonnes of CO_2 in 2013.

Even when food waste cannot be eliminated, its impacts can still be reduced, or even converted into benefits. For instance, animal by-products from slaughterhouses that are usually incinerated or disposed of in landfills can be treated by a new technology called the APRE process, which can treat 11 tonnes of dead animals every day, producing 4,000 m^3 of biogas (60% of which is methane) and 44 tonnes of liquid fertilizer. The heat generated can be turned into electricity to be used in production or sold on.

As we can see, many technological solutions to agri-food waste already exist and only need to be more effectively shared and affordably adapted to local contexts. However, as always, technology is only part of the answer—something that Paris retailer Intermarché creatively, humorously and profitably demonstrates with its recent Inglorious Fruits and Vegetables campaign, which discounts and celebrates fresh food that does not comply with EU size and colour restrictions and would otherwise have been dumped.

The sustainability revolution is as much about changing perceptions, attitudes and behaviours—the software—as about changing the technology.

Meeting water and energy challenges in the agri-food sector

Worldwide, the overall growth in demand for agricultural products will require a 140% increase in the supply of water over the next 20 years compared with the past 20 years. While the bulk of this demand will be from irrigation, food-processing plants can also be water intensive. So, any technological innovations in the industry that save water are welcome.

One such innovation is by Mars Petcare, which has developed a recirculation system that reduces the potable water used for cooling in its pet food production process by 95% (European Commission, 2011). Waste-water is also down by 95% and gas by 35% through the use of a treatment method that keeps the water microbiologically stable.

In Brazil, water used in sugar cane processing has gone down from 5.6 to 1.83 cubic metres (m³) per tonne in recent years, due to improved technologies and practices in waste-water treatment.

Further reductions can be made by replacing the standard wet cane washing process with a new technique of dry cane washing. Costa Rican company Azucarera El Viejo SA has found that this switch has resulted in more than six million gallons of water being saved each day during the harvest season, netting savings of approximately $54,000 (£32,000).

Of course, in food processing, it is not only volume of water that is important, but also the quality of water effluent associated with the manufacturing process. In Brazil, sugar cane is partly processed into ethanol. Vinasse is a by-product of this process that pollutes water. Technological innovation shows that, while in Brazil emissions of 10–12 litres of vinasse per litre of ethanol are standard, levels of 6 litres can be achieved.

Other examples of innovative water quality solutions in the agri-foods sector are Briter-Water, which has been piloted in the EU and uses intensified bamboo-based phytoremediation for treating dairy and other food industry effluent; and the Vertical Green Biobed, developed by HEPIA, a school from the University of Applied Sciences of western Switzerland, to improve water treatment of agricultural effluents.

Besides water issues, agriculture is also very energy intensive, accounting for 7% of the world's greenhouse gas emissions, according to 2010 figures (Ecofys, 2010). Even carbon emissions associated only with direct energy use by the sector stand at 1.4% of the world's total. Energy efficiency technologies will certainly help, but there is an equally big innovation opportunity in generating energy from agricultural waste.

It is estimated that the global biofuels market could double to $185.3 billion (£110.5 billion) by 2021 and that next generation sugar cane bagasse-to-biofuels technologies could expand ethanol production in key markets such as Brazil and India by 35% without land or water intensification. Experiences in this rapidly growing industry suggest three lessons which can be applied to sustainable technology innovation more generally.

1. **Technologies must be ready-for-market**: there are always competing technological solutions at the Research and Development (R&D) phase, but a critical test is which ones are ready to scale commercially. In the case of cellulosic biofuel technologies, despite early research into wheat straw and corn stover, sugar cane biomass ended up being more commercially attractive to big investors such as Blue Sugars, Novozymes, Iogen, Beta Renewables, DSM and Codexis.

2. **Partnership is critical for success**: there have been few standalone projects announced. Instead, technology companies from the US and the EU have generally teamed up with large aggregators of bagasse such as Raizen and Petrobras. Apart from technology transfer benefits, access to already-aggregated bagasse is economically essential.

3. **Policy support and market demand attract investment**: Brazil is especially attractive as a technology transfer destination due to a combination of policy certainty and strong ethanol demand. This combination is also stimulating parallel next generation biofuels.

Most notably GraalBio and Praj have significant projects targeting other feedstocks such as straw.

Investment in biofuels can also generate significant economic value for agri-food processors. During the sugar cane harvest, the left over fibre is burned and converted into energy via bagasse-to-biogas production. During the 2011/12 harvest, approximately 38 million kWh of energy derived from bagasse-to-biogas production was sold by Azucarera El Viejo to the Costa Rican Electricity Institute, bringing over $3 million (£1.79 million) of income to the company.

In Nepal, the Biogas Support programme installed over 250,000 domestic biogas plants in rural households between 1992 and 2011, using cattle manure to provide biogas for cooking and lighting, replacing traditional energy sources such as fuelwood, agricultural residue and dung. Besides health benefits from less indoor smoke, the project has cut 625,000 tonnes of CO_2.

And in Rwanda, there is a proposal—yet to be approved and implemented—for two biofuels companies, Eco-fuels Global and Eco Positive, to invest $250 million (£149 million) and grow 120 million jatropha trees, helping to make Rwanda self-reliant in biodiesel by 2025 and bringing jobs to 122 small oil-seed-producing co-operatives with over 12,000 members.

Sustainable tech in Africa: a case study

To understand the potential impact of sustainable technologies and why their adoption is often difficult, especially in developing countries, it is helpful to examine a specific case study.

C:AVA, the Cassava: Adding Value for Africa Project, promotes the production of High Quality Cassava Flour (HQCF) as an alternative for starch and other imported materials such as wheat flour. C:AVA has developed value chains for HQCF in Ghana, Tanzania, Uganda, Nigeria and Malawi aiming to improve the livelihoods and incomes of at least 90,000 smallholder households, including women and disadvantaged groups.

The main opportunity for technology to make a difference is in the drying process. A flash dryer dries cassava mash very quickly, preventing fermentation. The flash dryers that were available in Nigeria before C:AVA's intervention were run on used motor oil or diesel and tended to be highly fuel inefficient and costly.

C:AVA—led by the Natural Resources Institute of the University of Greenwich, working with the Federal University of Agriculture Abeokuta, and the Bill and Melinda Gates Foundation—evaluated the traditional flash dryers in 2009. Since then, they have introduced more efficient technology (double cyclone flash dryers). These involve heat exchange systems—using "waste" heat from one part of the process to feed into another part—better insulation and faster drying speeds. The efficiencies have improved the diesel fuel to flour production ratio by a factor of 18 according to C:AVA tests, reducing costs and CO_2 emissions.

However, these achievements have not been easy. Over the last five years, C:AVA has learned ten crucial lessons about the successful diffusion of more sustainable technologies in Africa:

1. **Capacity building**: a critical part of the technology transfer process was that C:AVA mentored a Nigerian fabricator to produce a flash dryer that meets international standards. As a result, new engineering knowledge and skills are being developed and embedded locally.

2. **Regional trade and infrastructure**: C:AVA organized experience sharing visits between cassava stakeholders in western and eastern Africa. Transporting a flash dryer from Nigeria to Malawi revealed significant constraints to technology transfer in the region due to poor transport infrastructure and high transaction costs (bureaucratic red tape).

3. **Value chain fluctuations**: technology can improve one part of the value chain, but changes in other parts can neutralize these benefits. For example, prices of fresh cassava roots can vary by more than 300% in one season. So C:AVA is also working with others to ensure that farmers obtain higher yield per unit area of cassava.

4. **Macro trends**: it is critical to monitor how changes in the macro environment could impact the technology investment. In Malawi, C:AVA identified large markets for HQCF and organized raw materials in anticipation of the introduction of artificial drying. But due to a drought, cassava suddenly became a major primary food in a predominantly maize consuming nation, resulting in a raw materials shortage.

5. **Working with investors**: the new dryers required investors willing to make an investment of $200,000 (£120,600). This difficulty

was overcome by addressing the fuel inefficiency of the traditional flash dryers, and working with potential investors on their business plans, identifying market opportunities and raw materials supply.

6. **Finance-dependent delays:** for C:AVA, almost all project targets that were dependent on private investor decision-making have been off-course. Technology projects need to include or seek guidance from private-sector partners in determining their expectations and fixing their decision-making time-lines within project cycles.

7. **Expectations management:** the perception that technology interventions will bring financial or tangible handouts can lead to disappointment and even hostility from potential beneficiaries when these expectations are not met. This can be exacerbated by development agencies providing short-term donations.

8. **Policy support:** C:AVA benefited from a favourable government policy environment in Nigeria, particularly in the period between 2002 and 2007 when the Presidential Initiative on Cassava was in operation. Currently, the Cassava Transformation Programme of the federal government provides another favourable environment to promote the technology.

9. **Private-sector partners:** one of the big lessons from C:AVA was that their set of collaborative partnerships, although well balanced in other respects, lacked private-sector representation. As a result, when it came to getting access to capital, the technology adoption time was considerably delayed.

10. **Spreading the benefits:** to scale the positive impact, there are plans for spreading the more efficient flash dryer technology through south–south investments (between developing countries). To this end, the Gates Foundation has funded demonstration projects in four additional countries, including Malawi, Ghana, Tanzania and Uganda.

Why banning dangerous chemicals is not enough

Let's turn our attention to another industry now: chemicals. To feed the world's chemical addiction, production has had to grow rapidly over the last 40 years. Are companies doing enough to make products and processes safer for humans and the environment?

The growth in chemical production in the past 40 years has been nothing short of explosive, with global output of $171 billion in 1970 burgeoning to more than $4 trillion in 2010 (an increase of more than 2,000%). By 2050, the market is expected to expand further to more than $14 trillion (an increase of more than 250% from 2010), with the BRICS countries dominating and accounting for more than $6 trillion together ($4 trillion for China alone).

The message is clear: this is not an industry that is going away. We are all, with our modern lifestyles, totally hooked on chemicals, whether for energy (petrochemicals), colourants (paints, inks, dyes, pigments), food production (fertilizers, pesticides), health (medicines, soaps, detergents) or beauty (perfumes, cosmetics).

Yet, like all drugs, chemicals have some serious side-effects. The World Health Organization (WHO) estimates that the chemical industry causes around a million deaths and 21 million disability adjusted life years (DALYs) globally every year (based on 2004 data). DALYs are a measure of overall disease burden, expressed as the number of years lost due to ill-health, disability or early death.

The main cause of these serious health impacts are acute poisoning, occupational exposure and lead in the environment. What's more, these WHO figures are almost certainly an underestimate, since they exclude (due to incomplete data) chronic consumer exposure to chemicals and chronic exposure to pesticides and heavy metals such as cadmium and mercury.

So here is the dilemma: chemicals are harming people—and even killing some—yet because of their benefits and the world's addiction, they cannot be eliminated, even if the renewable energy and organic farming sectors continue their boom of recent years. Taking this as a starting point, the next question becomes: what has the chemical industry done to make its products and processes less hazardous?

The industry has a self-regulatory programme called Responsible Care, which was created in 1985. According to the International Council of Chemical Associations' (ICCA) decennial report on progress in 2012, 85% of the world's leading global chemical companies have already signed up to its Global Charter. The ICCA can show significant improvements since 2002 in fatalities, injuries, carbon intensity and transportation incidents. Other impacts, such as water consumption, energy use and total carbon emissions, are still heading in the wrong direction.

All this is part of ICCA's contribution to the UN's Strategic Approach to International Chemicals Management (SAICM), which aims to achieve "sound chemical management" and to "minimise significant adverse impacts on the environment and human health" by 2020. That sounds good. But is it working? The data suggests we have a long way to go.

For example, in North America alone, 4.9 million metric tons of chemicals are released annually into the environment or disposed of, according to 2009 figures. This includes nearly 1.5 million metric tons of chemicals that are persistent, bioaccumulative and toxic, more than 756,000 metric tons of known or suspected carcinogens and nearly 667,000 metric tons of chemicals that are considered reproductive or developmental toxicants.

Besides the health impacts of these emissions, the disruptive effects of chemical pollution on ecosystems also have significant economic consequences. The cost to the global economy of chemical pollution has been estimated at $546 billion. This is projected to rise to $1.9 trillion by 2050, or 1.2% of global GDP. Of these externalities, 57% are associated with listed companies and their supply chains, and $314 billion can be attributed to the largest 3,000 public companies in the world.

Scary numbers, but the chemicals sector says everything is under control. They are aware of the problems and are dealing with them, multilaterally and as a sector, through a plethora of initiatives—such as the Basel, Rotterdam and Stockholm Conventions, the US Toxic Release Inventory and the EU Registration, Evaluation, Authorisation and Restriction of Chemicals programme. The ICCA's Chemicals Portal also offers free public access to product stewardship information. To date, product safety summaries are available for close to 3,500 chemicals.

And besides these collective efforts, most large companies now also have lists of chemicals they ban and those they prefer, such as Nike's Considered Chemistry, Boots' Priority Substances List, S.C. Johnson's Greenlist and Sony's Green Partners Standards. However, the issue is that these are defensive actions, a bit like trying to lock up a fierce lion in a cage, rather than taming it—or better still, exchanging it for a pet cat or dog.

Can the chemical sector ever be sustainable? The answer is maybe. The big leap forward—with a tantalizing promise of not only making chemicals safer or "less bad", but potentially harmless or even "good"—is the emerging green chemistry industry.

Will green chemistry save us from toxification?

A swath of green chemistry initiatives could revolutionize the industry but just taking the toxic stuff out isn't the answer; ingredients and design need to change.

The "green" label has been so abused over the past few decades that it is wise to suspect PR spin (what many call "greenwashing"). In the case of green chemicals, however, there is at least some serious thinking and extensive application to back up its claims.

Let's start with what it means. The OECD defines green chemistry as "the design, manufacture and use of efficient, effective, safe and more environmentally benign chemical products and processes". More specifically, green chemistry should use fewer hazardous and harmful feedstocks and reagents, improve the energy and material efficiency of chemical processes, use renewable feedstocks or wastes in preference to fossil fuels or mined resources and design chemical products for better re-use or recycling.

Popular categories of green chemistry include biochemical fuel cells, biodegradable packaging, aqueous solvents, white biotechnology (the application of biotechnology for industrial purposes), totally chlorine-free bleaching technologies and green plastics.

One research report suggests that the green chemistry market will grow from $2.8 billion in 2011 to $98.5 billion by 2020 and will save the industry $65.5 billion through direct cost savings and avoided liability for environmental and social impacts. Others are even more bullish, predicting growth in the bio-based chemicals market from $78 billion in 2012 to $198 billion by 2017, eventually accounting for 50% of the chemicals market by 2050.

But can we trust green chemistry? One way to check is the US Environmental Protection Agency's Design for the Environment (DfE) Safer Product Labelling Program. The Safer Chemical Ingredients List contains chemicals that have been screened to exclude CMRs (carcinogens, reproductive/developmental toxicants and mutagens) and PBTs (persistent, bioaccumulative, and toxic compounds) and other chemicals of concern.

At present, about 2,500 products carry the DfE Safer Product Label, with compliance verified by certifiers such as NSF Sustainability. Beyond this, there are a host of multi-stakeholder initiatives that give further guidance, checks and validity to claims, including Clean Production Action's GreenScreen, GreenBlue's CleanGredients and iSustain's Alliance Assessment.

All these hazardous chemical screening lists may seem like striving for "less bad" rather than "good", but they are also sparking innovations around the world. Imagine what would happen if we substituted all our fossil fuel derived plastics with Brazilian company Braskem's sugarcane ethanol derived Bio-PE (polyethylene) and Bio-PP (polypropylene), which removes up to 2.15 metric tons of CO_2 for each ton produced.

What if many of the plastics used in the automotive sector were replaced by a new latex-free material produced through a dry powder coating technology by French project Latexfri? Or perhaps we could move to starches created by Ethiopian company YASCAI from *enset*, a local plant?

Another approach, which UNIDO has been promoting, is to move towards chemical leasing, where chemical manufacturers take responsibility for the safe recovery and disposal of the chemicals they sell. For example, in Colombia, a chemical leasing programme between Ecopetrol and Nalco de Colombia resulted in a reduction of the costs of the treatment process by almost 20%, with savings of $1.8 million for Ecopetrol and $463,000 for Nalco.

In Sri Lanka, chemical leasing between Wijeya Newspapers and General Ink resulted in ink savings of around 15,000 kg, equivalent to approximately $50,000 per year. In Egypt, Delta Electrical Appliances, Akzo Nobel Powder Coating and Chemetall Italy reduced consumption of chemicals for pretreatment chemicals by 15–20% and for powder coating by 50% as a result of chemical leasing.

Will all of these green chemistry initiatives revolutionize the industry? Cradle to Cradle (Braungart and McDonough, 2008), previously mentioned, hopes to do just that. Co-founder and German chemist, Michael Braungart, told me that in 1987 when he was analysing complex household products, he identified 4,360 different chemicals in a TV set and concluded that "it doesn't help just to take any toxic stuff out of it". Rather, products have to be redesigned so that all inputs are either biological nutrients (that can harmlessly biodegrade) or technical nutrients (that can be endlessly and safely recycled).

So does Cradle to Cradle represent the cutting edge of green chemistry? In *The Top 50 Sustainability Books* (Visser and CPSL, 2009), Braungart says:

> I'm just talking about good chemistry. Chemistry is not good when the chemicals accumulate in the biosphere; that's just stupid. Young scientists immediately understand that a chemical is not good when it accumulates in mother's breast milk. It's just primitive chemistry. So now we can make far better chemistry, far better material science, far better physics.

Lessons from Egypt in building a cleaner chemicals industry

So far, I have looked at the impacts of the chemicals sector and innovations such as green chemistry. But how do we share the technologies that are making the chemicals sector more sustainable, especially in rapidly emerging countries?

To answer this question, I'm going to shine the spotlight on Egypt—where factories are discharging 2.5 million cubic metres of untreated effluent into the rivers every day, much of it laced with toxic chemicals. The country also faces a water and energy crisis. But three Egyptian companies are tackling these environmental issues through technology adoption and transfer.

The first is Arab Steel Fabrication Company (El Sewedy), which has applied a technological solution to recover hydrochloric acid from its galvanization process. Besides the obvious environmental benefits, the company is saving 345,000 Egyptian pounds (£30,000) a year. The second company, Mac Carpet, has used technology to create an automatic system for recycling of thickener agents, which saves it about EGP5 million per year.

The third case is El Obour for Paints and Chemical Industries (Pachin), which manufactures paints, inks and resins. Like many chemical companies, the manufacturing process is very energy intensive. As part of a government programme to promote renewable energy in Egypt (part-funded by the EU), a technology company in Germany has installed solar collectors at the Pachin facility. These heat the water to 65 degrees Celsius, then by using a heat exchanger, recover the heat and use it to keep the fatty acid store at an optimal temperature, saving the company EGP100,000 a year.

In all three cases, there are eight lessons to be learned.

1. **Economic drivers**: when asked about the top three benefits from implementing sustainable technology, El Sewedy and Mac Carpet Company both mentioned resource productivity and economic development. Environmental improvement was also a key factor (in the top three for both), but would have been insufficient on its own to motivate the technology change.

2. **Skills development**: significant barriers to technology adoption for both companies were the lack of local qualified workers and institutional capacity. To overcome this, the technology provider and the Egyptian National Cleaner Production Centre (ENCPC) had to do training. Ali Abo Sena, an ENCPC representative, said

that education was needed not only on the specific technologies, but also more broadly on the seriousness of the water crisis in Egypt.

3. **Business continuity**: for Pachin, energy consumption is not just an environmental issue, but one that is business critical. In 2013, the Egyptian government announced planned to ration subsidies for petrol and diesel fuel, and hiked fuel prices for heavy industry by 33% at the beginning of the year. Power outages have become more commonplace, resulting in significant disruption to business continuity and loss of economic value.

4. **Market potential**: the German solar company was prepared to part-fund, install and support the technology transfer to Pachin in Egypt because it enabled them to show a working demonstration of a project in a market that has massive potential for the business. The marketing benefits of sustainable technology in developing countries should not be underestimated.

5. **Macro conditions**: it is unlikely that the Pachin project would have been embraced so enthusiastically had Egypt not experienced an energy crisis—and accompanying rises in energy costs—in recent years. Although these macro conditions are beyond the control of sustainable technology providers, being sensitive to the opportunities that they can provide can help ensure that the correct markets are chosen for deployment.

6. **Financial support**: although long-term economic development is an important benefit of the adoption of sustainable technologies, the high initial cost of these projects and the relatively long payback period can be a significant barrier. In the case of Pachin, this was overcome by getting financial support for the project (from the EU and the technology provider).

7. **Plan for scaling**: a lack of qualified workers to install, operate and maintain Pachin's solar technology was overcome by providing the relevant skills training. However, in order to ensure future scaling, a plan was also devised for moving towards local manufacturing (possibly through a joint venture).

8. **Local adaptation**: the Egyptian National Cleaner Production Centre—working as an intermediary—determined that the German

solar technology was overengineered for the local conditions. In particular, since the technology was made in Germany and had to comply with EU specifications and perform in a region with ambient sunlight, it was found that the insulation materials could be replaced with less expensive substitutes, which performed adequately under local conditions.

Major reductions in the environmental impacts of the chemicals industry—as well as economic benefits—can be achieved by adopting and transferring existing best practice sustainable technologies. The problem, therefore, is not our lack of sustainable technologies, but our ability to finance, incentivize and build capacity for their deployment where they are most needed in the world.

Iron ore and rare earth metals mining: an industry under siege?

Let us turn now to a third industry sector, namely metals. Resource scarcity and human rights issues surrounding metals extraction, coupled with unrelenting global demand mean the industry is facing some tough realities.

The good news is that the number of people living in extreme poverty could drop from 1.2 billion in 2010 to under 100 million by 2050, according to UN projections. The bad news is that the flotilla of hope currently rising on the tide of economic growth in emerging countries is at serious risk of being dragged down under the waves. The reason is growing resource scarcity and the environmental disasters that could ensue.

As always, the poorest will be worst affected. The UNDP projects that, under an environmental disaster scenario, instead of reducing the population living in extreme poverty in south Asia from over half a billion to less than 100 million by 2050, it could rise to 1.2 billion. In sub-Saharan Africa, the numbers may rise from under 400 million to over a billion. For the world as a whole, an environmental disaster scenario could mean 3.1 billion more people living in extreme poverty in 2050, as compared with an accelerated development scenario.

The message is simple: unless these booming economies—and the high-income countries they churn out "widgets" for—can lighten the weighty anchor of resource consumption, we will all, sooner or later, get that sinking feeling. To illustrate the point, demand for steel—driven in no small part by a global car fleet doubling to 1.7 billion by 2030—is expected to increase by about 80% from 1.3 billion tonnes in 2010 to 2.3 billion tonnes in 2030. These trends raise red flags about material shortages of many metals in the future.

Besides steel, rare earth metals are cause for concern, as they comprise 17 chemical elements that are critical in the automotive, electronics and renewables sectors. Not only is demand for these metals rising, China is responsible for about 97% of global production. The United States, Japan and Germany are making big investments to secure their own supplies, but these new mining projects may take a decade to come on stream. As a result, supply shortages are predicted. Yet rare earth metal recycling rates remain very low—only 1% in Germany, for example.

Add the challenge of "conflict minerals"—and the metals sector starts to look like the Titanic. The metals of most concern right now are tantalum (or coltan), tin, tungsten and gold—collectively known as 3TG—which are used extensively in the electronics industry. The Democratic Republic of Congo (DRC) and adjoining countries have been the hot spots—and the target of legislation such as the Dodd-Frank Act in the US—but other conflict minerals can (and probably will) arise for other metals in other parts of the world in future.

Besides resource scarcity and human rights issues, the mining and metals industry has significant environmental impacts, especially on land, energy and water. Trucost estimated that the largest metals and mining companies of the world have environmental external costs of around $220 billion, 77% of which relate to greenhouse gases.

For iron ore, if carbon prices would rise to a level of $30 per tonne, iron ore costs would increase by 3.3% across the industry. An adequate incorporation of the water costs of iron ore mining would result in a 2.5% cost increase. Combining carbon and water costs, this could mean increased costs of up to 16% for some operators in water-scarce regions. These land, energy and water impacts also appear to be increasing, as about three times as much material needs to be moved for the same ore extraction as a century ago.

The picture that emerges is of a metals sector under siege, an industry that is soon to be the victim of its own success. And yet it is also one of the sectors that has the most potential for innovation and technological solutions. McKinsey estimate that iron and steel energy efficiency and end-use steel efficiency could deliver $278 billion in resource savings by 2030 and go some way towards addressing the metals scarcity crisis. The metals sector may still be in danger, but sustainable technologies could make the situation better.

Why metals should be recycled, not mined

There is no denying that the sustainability impacts of the extractive sector are serious—sometimes even tragic and catastrophic. But they are not without solutions. Technology, which is the source of so much destruction in the mining and metals industry, can also be its saviour.

The most obvious opportunity for the sector is to embrace the circular economy. Many metals can be recycled—and in some cases, actual recycling rates are already high. For example, according to research by Ecorys (2012), 67% of scrap steel, more than 60% of aluminium and 35% of copper (45–50% in the EU) is already recycled. Apart from resource savings, there is often also a net energy benefit. Energy accounts for 30% of primary aluminium production costs, but recycling of aluminium scrap uses only 5% of the energy of primary production.

Recyclability of metals is as important as recycling rates. We need more companies that grow the markets for recycled materials, such as Novelis, which announced the commercial availability of the industry's first independently certified, high-recycled-content aluminium (90% minimum) designed specifically for the beverage can market.

The opportunity to increase recycling rates is significant. Today, according to UNEP (2011), less than one third of 60 metals analysed have an end-of-life recycling rate above 50% and 34 elements are below 1%. The irony is that recycling is often far more efficient than mining. For example, a post-consumer automotive catalyst has a concentration of platinum group metals (such as platinum, palladium and rhodium) more than 100 times higher than in natural ores. Already, special refining plants are achieving recovery rates of more than 90% from this "waste" (UNEP and Öko-Institut, 2009).

This sustainability business case logic has not gone unnoticed. Given the importance of rare earth metals in electronics and renewable technologies, Japan has set aside ¥42 billion (£231 million) for the development of rare earth recycling, while Veolia Environmental Services says it plans to extract precious metals such as palladium from road dust in London (McKinsey, 2011).

Some recycling technologies are high tech. For example, the Saturn project in Germany uses sensor-based technologies for sorting and recovery of nonferrous metals. Similarly, Twincletoes is a technology collaboration between the UK, Italy and France that recovers steel fibres from end-of-life tyres and uses them as a reinforcing agent in concrete.

By contrast, E-Parisaraa, which is India's first government authorized electronic waste recycler, is much more low-tech, using manual dismantling and segregation by hand before shredding and density separation occur. This is a good reminder that the best available sustainable technology is not always the most applicable, especially in developing countries.

Recycling is not the only way for technology to reduce the impact of metals. If we look at energy consumption, each phase of the steelmaking process presents opportunities. For example, direct energy use can be reduced by 50% in the manufacture of coke and sinter through plant heat recovery, and the use of waste fuel and coal moisture control. In the rolling process, hot charging, recuperative burners and controlled oxygen levels can reduce the energy by 88% and electricity consumption by 5% (McKinsey, 2011).

Other technologies, such as using pulverized coal injection, top pressure recovery turbines and blast furnace control systems, can reduce direct energy use by 10% and electricity by 35%. In electric arc furnace steelmaking, improved process control, oxy fuel burners and scrap preheating can cut electricity consumption by 76%. In fact, applying these kinds of energy-saving technology could result in energy efficiency improvements in the steel sector of between 0.7% and 1.4% every year from 2010 to 2030 (McKinsey, 2011).

Water is another critical issue that suggests significant opportunities. For example, BHP Billiton's Olympic Dam in South Australia achieved industrial water efficiency improvements of 15%, from 1.27 kilolitres to 1.07 kilolitres per tonne of material milled. That may not sound like a lot, but when scaled across the operations of the world's fourth largest copper and gold source and the largest uranium source, it makes a huge difference.

Sometimes the technologies are fairly simple. In the metal finishing sector, improving rinsing efficiency represents the greatest water reduction option. For example, C & R Hard Chrome & Electrolysis Nickel Service switched its single-rinse tanks to a system of multiple counterflow rinse tanks, and installed restrictive flow nozzles on water inlets. As a result, the process line has reduced water consumption by 87% (NCDPPEA, 2009).

We can see, therefore, that technology can help to rescue the high-impact extractives sector from its siege by the forces of sustainability. However, it requires some critical shifts. Extractives companies need to recast themselves as resource stewardship companies—experts at circular production and post-consumer "mining". And customers and governments need to give up their compulsive throw-away habits and embrace the take-back economy.

Closing the loop on steel

In the next few decades, as resource scarcity starts to bite, and resource prices steadily climb, mining and metals companies will be forced to shapeshift from primary extractors to secondary recyclers. Necessity, rather than an unexpected attack of conscience, will be the driving force behind this transition to a circular economy. So let's look at some lessons from the sector most ripe for revolution, namely the steel industry.

According to the World Steel Association (2014), in 2013, world crude steel production totalled 1.6 billion tonnes and employed 50 million people, either directly or indirectly. The industry is vocal in its support for sustainable development, claiming that—despite massive growth in demand—the amount of energy required to produce a tonne of steel has been reduced by 50% in the past 30 years.

A far stronger virtue in its pursuit of sustainability is that steel is 100% recyclable and backed by an impressive business case: more than 1,400 kg of iron ore, 740 kg of coal, and 120 kg of limestone are saved for every tonne of steel scrap made into new steel (World Steel Association, 2014). It is puzzling, therefore, that usage of scrap steel in 2013 was still only around 580 million tonnes (Bureau of International Recycling, 2014). Why is closing the loop on steel so difficult?

Lessons can be learned from Adelca, an Ecuadorian steel manufacturer that is trying to blaze a trail for the circular economy in Latin America. According to the Latin American Steel Association (Alacero, 2014), Ecuador is still a relatively small player, making up about 1% of the Latin American crude steel market, which is dominated by Brazil at 53% and Mexico at 27% (ranked nine and 13 respectively in the world market).

Adelca supplies Ecuador, Venezuela, Colombia, Peru and Chile with a variety of rolled and stretched steel products. Before 2008, Adelca was importing billets (a narrow, generally square, bar of steel) from China and elsewhere, but after analysing the economic and environmental benefits, the company decided to invest in an electric arc furnace (EAF) and start recycling metal scrap in order to make products for the construction sector.

The first part of Adelca's sustainable technology solution was to install the EAF, thus allowing it to make its own steel billets from recycled scrap steel. According to Isabel Meza (2013), head of integrated management at Adelca, by importing fewer billets, they are saving $12 million (£7.6 million) on the 20,000 tonnes of steel they produce every month. Apart from using fewer mineral resources, each tonne of recycled steel uses 40% less water, 75% less energy and generates 1.28 tonnes less solid waste than steel from raw materials. There is also an 86% reduction in air emissions and a 76% reduction in water pollution (World Economic Forum, 2009).

The second part of Adelca's sustainable technology solution was to help to stimulate and organize the metals recycling sector in Ecuador, since it does not have enough supply of scrap metal to meet its own steel production demand. Today, Adelca's Recyclers Network generates about 4,000 jobs (direct and indirect), with income exceeding $1 million (£637,000) a month. Also, the steelworks, scrap iron preparation process, transportation system and complementary services generate more than 1,500 direct jobs for 50 small companies. Although Adelca still imports $80 million (£51 million) a year in raw materials, it estimates it contributes $120 million (£76.5 million) a year to the national economy just from the avoided imports.

The third part of Adelca's sustainable technology solution was to install a bio-digester that turns the company's organic waste into methane gas for community use, as well as to generate fertilizer for local crops. Although the financial savings are not big at about $35 (£22) a day in energy savings for the community and $100 (£63) in waste disposal costs for the company, there is a significant pay-off in terms of "social licence to operate", i.e. improved community relations.

Let's look at four lessons Adelca has learned about applying sustainable technology.

1. **Financial returns**: the EAF technology was bought from the US and funded by taking a substantial mortgage from the bank. Commercially, the scale of the investment represented a significant risk, but the expected financial returns from the technology allowed the company to take this risk. Environmental benefits alone would not have sufficed.

2. **Community education**: Adelca lost eight months in delayed production due to community resistance to the EAF. The community feared that the heat, power and radiation from the furnace would endanger the health of the community, and that its heavy electricity demands would negatively affect the community's own supply. Despite being unfounded, these fears required a substantial and expensive education effort to gain a social licence to operate.

3. **Supplier relations**: since Adelca's demand for scrap metals is greater than the supply—and recycled scrap costs less than imported billets—the company has invested in building up its

network of recyclers, including donating metal cutting equipment, offering loans, providing and paying for training and promising the best price for the scrap metals provided.

4. **Marketing benefits:** by investing in sustainable technologies, Adelca has differentiated itself in the market. In its public corporate mission, it is able to claim to be "leaders on recycling for the steel production, with excellence in ... environmental protection and social responsibility". This commitment helped it to become the first Ecuadorian company to achieve the Latin American S2M certification for corporate responsibility and sustainability.

The Adelca case shows us why the resource revolution is worthwhile, yet still so slow in happening. The positive impacts on manufacturing and natural capital are clear, but challenges remain in getting access to financial capital and ensuring the human and social capital benefits are effectively communicated.

Eco-innovation: beyond creating technology for technology's sake

Despite the challenges, slowly but surely, sustainable technologies are being applied by business and transforming our outdated industrial model, which is no longer fit for purpose. As examples from the agri-food, chemicals and metals sectors have shown, removing barriers to the sharing of existing technologies is just as important as coming up with new and better tools. So how does this work in practice?

When working with sustainable technologies, companies must decide whether to collaborate or go it alone. This decision should be based on an assessment of a company's in-house competences, technical readiness and capacity.

BeniSweif is a small engineering company in Egypt that produces coloured pigments for the metals industry. With the support of the Egyptian National Cleaner Production Centre (NCPC), the company invented a new yellow iron oxide-derived pigment in a process that allowed them to recover hydrochloric acid with a concentration of 25%, which can be used again (Abo Sena, 2014). The new product sells for almost five times the production cost. This development has created a new business model, with clear financial and environmental benefits.

Similarly, Jiangsu Redbud Textile Technology entered into a technology transfer agreement with the governments of Benin, Mali and others to promote jute fibre-green technology (SS-GATE, 2010). The Chinese company developed and tested new varieties of jute, which are 100% recyclable and well adapted to wastelands, saline ground, low-lying wetlands and drought conditions. Now a collaborative platform, SS-GATE, is introducing this technology into Africa. The product was created to fit environmental conditions, and the institution created a collaborative space for innovation.

Another example is the series of XPRIZE awards, which help teams from across the world to compete for funding by solving a specific social, technical or environmental challenge. For instance, the $2 million Wendy Schmidt Ocean Health XPRIZE promises to improve our understanding of how CO_2 emissions are affecting ocean acidification by encouraging teams to design sensors that can help us begin the process of healing our oceans. Similarly, a Carbon XPRIZE has been proposed with the goal to develop radical new technologies and products that make capturing CO_2 from power plants a source of profit rather than a liability. This is typical of open innovation for sustainability.

These are the kinds of case being studied in a European Commission-funded research programme on eco-innovation (UNEP, 2015). The programme is looking at methods for the identification, development, transfer and adaptation of technologies to further sustainable development. The aim is to develop local capacity and resources for eco-innovation in developing and emerging economies, especially through supporting intermediaries such as the National Cleaner Production Centres.

The UNEP (United Nations Environment Programme) report on the business case for eco-innovation is an example of the results of the programme. Eco-innovation—as distinct from eco-efficiency—has emerged from the realization that without innovation we are unlikely to solve many of our global social and environmental challenges, from poverty to climate change.

According to the Philips Meaningful Innovation Index, "There is an appetite for future innovations to go beyond creating technology for technology's sake, instead aiming to make a difference in people's everyday lives." Hence technology is an enabler for eco-innovation, not only in terms of physical equipment and tools but also in the knowledge, techniques and skills that surround its deployment and use.

Technology can be a catalyst for different aspects of the eco-innovation process, as well as being a marketable product or outcome of eco-innovation itself. Eco-innovators push the boundaries of their companies. By modifying products, processes and organizational structures, eco-innovation improves sustainability performance and competitiveness.

Eco-innovation is the next evolution beyond eco-efficiency. Whereas eco-efficiency tends to be focused on productivity and the impact of single technologies or individual steps in the business process, eco-innovation looks to strategically transform the whole business model. When it comes to reinventing capitalism, eco-innovation is one of the next waves business will want to surf if it is to survive and thrive.

4
Unlocking change through corporate transparency

Trends in corporate accountability

Information has never been more readily available. Technology presents citizens with far greater opportunities to engage with sustainability issues than ever before. Corporations are more actively courting the views of stakeholders online and are also increasingly expected to disclose their performance to interested and affected parties, as well as to contribute towards an ongoing dialogue.

Against this backdrop, my think-tank consultancy, Kaleidoscope Futures, sought to ascertain the key trends related to corporate reporting, sustainability ratings and crowdsourced information.[1] In the two chapters that follow, I present the main findings, including the following ten trends:

Trend 1: There is explosive sustainability reporting growth, but from an extremely low base.

Trend 2: We see a proliferation of reporting standards, with mandatory disclosure on the rise.

---

1   This research was conducted for Wikirate and summarized in Kaleidoscope Futures (2015) Transforming corporate accountability: the revolutions of transparency, ratings and social media. Report. London: Kaleidoscope Futures. The following two chapters are based on this report. I am grateful to the Kaleidoscope Futures team, especially Scott Walker, Azadeh Ardakani and Amos Doornbos, for their contributions to its content.

Trend 3: There is improvement of data quantity and quality, driven by emerging information technologies.

Trend 4: There is a shift from corporate to value chain data, with traceability becoming the new watchword.

Trend 5: We are seeing the increasing importance of sustainability ratings, as a driver of sustainability performance.

Trend 6: We should expect a consolidation of sustainability ratings agencies, due to competition and questionnaire fatigue.

Trend 7: There is a rising demand for more transparency by rating agencies, to counter low levels of trust.

Trend 8: There is a drive for social media to go beyond being used as a marketing channel to being used an action research database.

Trend 9: We see the growing use of crowdsourcing as a stakeholder engagement tool, allowing proactive anticipation of issues.

Trend 10: We are witnessing a transformation of the power of connection into the power of collaboration.

In addition, I share more details about the following five insights:

Insight 1: Hyper-connectivity makes responsiveness more possible—and less likely.

Insight 2: Value–action gaps make stakeholder feedback more collectable—yet less valuable.

Insight 3: The wisdom of the crowd can, without validation, also become the tragedy of the commons.

Insight 4: The openness of open source is questionable when values are a filter.

Insight 5: Questions remain about accountability ratings when the guardians are not guarded.

Explosive sustainability reporting growth

Since reporting on sustainability began in the early 1990s, catalysed by the disclosure requirements of the EU Eco-Management and Auditing Scheme (EMAS) and subsequently promoted by the Global Reporting Initiative (GRI) and other institutions and standards, it has continued to gain momentum and is set to continue into the future.

Now, according to Corporate Register, there are at least 54,585 corporate responsibility reports, across 10,980 companies, in over 161 countries—an exponential increase on 2008 levels (3,000 reports). The 2013 Grant Thornton international business report, a global survey of 3,300 businesses in 44 economies indicates that one third issue corporate responsibility reports (Grant Thornton, 2013).

Despite this impressive growth, however, the number of companies reporting on sustainability remains a tiny minority. Generally, it is only large, high-profile, branded companies (above 500 employees) that have the incentives and resources to report any information.

According to a recent Bloomberg analysis of 25,000 companies, three quarters did not report any sustainability performance information (Corporate Sustainability Reporting Coalition, 2013). Viewed against World Bank estimates of 120 million companies globally, the numbers of sustainability reporters are minuscule.

The 2014 KPMG Survey of Corporate Responsibility Reporting indicates that the Americas have now overtaken Europe as the leading reporting region, largely due to an increase in reporting in Latin America: 76% of (large) companies in the Americas now report, as compared to 73% in Europe and 71% in the Asia–Pacific region (KPMG, 2014).

While businesses are generally enthusiastic to promote positive performance they have achieved, transparency tends to be rather more limited when it comes to describing their failures or ongoing challenges. Some corporate reports are validated via third-party assurance, but many are not, although statistics do point to an upward trend.

Overall, the increasing level of corporate transparency (from a very low base) is significant. Furthermore, the wave of transparency is expected to continue over the next decade, especially as more emerging economies come into line with international norms and stakeholder expectations.

Proliferation of reporting standards

Although more corporate sustainability reporting is taking place, this is being done against diverse issues, with different national, sector and international standards and indices being used. A 2013 review of 30 countries found over 140 national sustainability disclosure standards, of which two thirds were mandatory (KPMG, 2013). New changes—driven by political interests—continue to appear at both national and multilateral levels.

For example, India's new Companies Bill has made CSR mandatory for large companies, thereby imposing legal reporting requirements on around 16,000 businesses. And in 2014, the EU agreed to amend existing accounting legislation to require "public interest companies" with more than 500 employees to report on social, environmental and diversity matters. We expect further developments in national regulatory frameworks to shape the transparency landscape and "force" companies to report in the future.

Besides mandatory reporting, market forces are already providing de facto regulatory pressures, with stock markets contributing to the multitude of reporting standards. Reporting on specific "material" issues is increasingly necessary for companies making statements in their reports to investors and regulatory filings. Many of these disclosures are typically boiler-plate warnings about risks from legal action or natural disasters, but represent an important trend nevertheless.

In terms of voluntary standards, the Global Reporting Initiative (GRI) Sustainability Reporting Guidelines (now in their fourth edition, called G4) are already well established and widely adopted. GRI has also issued several sector supplements, as has the Sustainability Accounting Standards Board (SASB). This trend towards sector-specific reporting will likely continue.

In contrast to the GRI, the International Integrated Reporting Committee (IIRC) is pushing for the annual financial report and the sustainability report to become integrated. Its International Framework was published in December 2013; hence, it is still too early to tell whether integrated reporting will become the norm, and if so, how long the transition process may take.

While reporting against specific standards has increased, on the downside, the vast proliferation and diversification of standards has also led to market confusion at the investor and consumer levels. A simple way to describe the repercussions could be "more noise, less signal". According to Mark Tulay, Program Manager at Global Initiative for Sustainability Ratings (GISR), "there are over 600 ways to describe the issues affecting corporate sustainability; there are over 1,500 indicators that express and measure this" (Kaleidoscope Futures, 2015).

What is missing across the standards arena, therefore, is greater clarity and more co-ordination. It is hoped that, over time, convergence may, and should, occur among the GRI, SASB, the IIRC, as well as other reporting frameworks such as the Carbon Disclosure Project (CDP). Arguably, the global reporting community wants to see fewer but more material disclosures on ESG (environmental, social and governance). But even if convergence does occur, the question of discerning performance excellence still remains fluid.

Improvement of data quantity and quality

The tools that companies use to report on sustainability remain rudimentary—primitive even—compared with those used for financial disclosure. Five years ago, very few companies were taking advantage of innovative technology to report related information. In 2009, a GRI (2009) survey found no companies using XBRL to tag data or Web 2.0 technologies to create engagement and dialogue with users of their primary report.

Even by 2013, only 37% of companies surveyed by EY (2013) used a centralized database system for environmental data management, while only 8% used packaged software for social and governance data.

Nevertheless, progress is being made. GRI has worked with Deloitte to establish an XBRL taxonomy for ESG metrics. In the US, the SEC requires XBRL tagging of financial data according to mature taxonomies. This will expand the definition of integrated reporting well beyond the scope of company-generated reports published once yearly. Now that Bloomberg has entered the fray, it is only a matter of time before users can do their own data integration in real time.

Notwithstanding the immaturity of sustainability reporting tools, a significant amount of quantitative nonfinancial data is streaming into the public domain. It is inevitable that advances in "big data" analytics will start to be applied to these sustainability databases. "Data volumes and databases are getting much larger," says Pratap Chatterjee, Executive Director of CorpWatch, "assisted by the significant increase in data automation" (Kaleidoscope Futures, 2015).

Hence, data structuring, searchability and sign-posting will become at least as important as weaving a qualitative narrative.

Shift from corporate to value chain data

As the value chains of global corporations become larger, longer and more complex, there is growing demand by civil society organizations, governments and customers for disclosures on the sustainability impacts on (and of) suppliers, as well as the social and environmental impacts of products and services across their entire life-cycle.

There are certainly trends towards companies increasingly exposing internal data sets to selected stakeholders. Information is being published through a combination of online data repositories and continuous releases of news to a self-selected group of users.

David Siegel, author of *Pull* (Siegel, 2010), a book on the power of the semantic web, calls this a change from a "lead–push" to a "pull–follow" model of transparency, whereby stakeholders can interrogate fractal (multilevel) corporate performance data. He predicts that over the next 10–20 years it will change business's interactions with users. But the pace of change will depend on several variables, including the semantic web infrastructure that is put in place, among many other factors.

The Transparent Economy report by Volans and GRI (2010) predicts that: "Sustainability reporting will increasingly build on a database of ESG information and data, packaged in different formats, with different stories, using different communications channels and media, in order to match the diversity of stakeholders' expectations."

Raw data alone presents its own challenges. While quantities of information are soaring, analysing it, spotting patterns and extracting useful information will conversely become harder. What really matters in the future is how it is organized and made accessible. No doubt, big data can potentially have a massive impact when analysed and presented correctly. Hence, we can expect more calls from stakeholders for data, both public and private, to be made far more readily available.

There is some irony here. Over the past decades, the production of commodities has globalized at a staggering pace, and yet our knowledge about the production of those same commodities has actually shrunk. SustainAbility (2011a) observes in their Signed, Sealed … Delivered? report that "a key transparency trend relates to the traceability of products through their entire life cycle with strong arguments put forward that the sustainability movement needs to deconstruct and evolve the old model that combines standards, certification and on-pack marks".

Among the pioneers of product-level sustainability reporting are Patagonia, which launched their Footprint Chronicles in 2007. Walmart, although not a leader on transparency, gave a significant boost to supply chain reporting when, in 2009, they announced their intention to create a "worldwide sustainable product index" to screen their 100,000 suppliers.

Sustainability Director at Interface, Ramon Arratia, believes "full product transparency" using life-cycle assessment allows consumers to see where the greatest positive difference can be made (Kaleidoscope Futures, 2015). Accordingly, he and others call for more benchmarking to provide real transparency, thereby allowing customers to make meaningful comparisons in their purchasing decisions.

A number of organizations already do important work in this space, such as Good Guide and We Green, making information on products and supply chains available to people when they purchase or invest.

In 2013, according to the KPMG (2014) survey of corporate responsibility reporting, 73% of European companies in the Global Fortune 250 reported in detail on the impacts of their products and services, with US (49%) and Asia–Pacific (32%) companies lagging further behind.

One instructive case in this area is Nike's "Making" App. The app is powered by the Nike Materials Sustainability Index (MSI), a database that was created by Nike over a seven-year period, using publicly available data on the environmental impacts of materials. The first release of Making includes the 22 materials that are most commonly used in apparel and home goods. It will continue to evolve, with the next iteration including materials that are relevant for footwear designers.

All materials in Making have a Material Score that aggregates environmental impacts in four key areas: chemistry, energy or greenhouse gas intensity, water or land intensity, and physical waste. The higher the score, the better the environmental footprint of the material. Making also allows users to rank materials by each of the four key impact areas. Scores for each impact area are calculated based on specific indicators.

Increasing importance of sustainability ratings

Sustainability reporting by business—whether at corporate or product level—is only one face of the transparency coin. On the other side, we find sustainability ratings produced by third parties to assess the performance of companies. The development of ethical investment funds and indexes—from the early pioneering work of the Pax World Fund and Domini Social Index through to FTSE4Good and the Dow Jones Sustainability Indexes—has resulted in the growth in the number and sophistication of sustainability ratings around the world.

Eric Whan, Director of GlobeScan's sustainability practice, believes that "ratings will become more important, more numerous and more mainstream over time" (Kaleidoscope Futures, 2015). This conclusion is supported by SustainAbility's (2013) Rate the Raters report, which found that 51% of sustainability experts think ratings are more important than they were three years ago in driving corporate sustainability performance, while 63% believe they will be more important three years from now.

In fact, SustainAbility's (2010) Rate the Raters research analysis identified over 100 rating systems already in existence. These provide a critical counterbalance to sustainability reporting, since independent third parties typically administer ratings.

Darby Hobbs, CEO of Social 3, suggests that, "in the next five to eight years you'll see a lot more momentum in the sustainability ratings arena". Furthermore, says Mark Tulay, Program Manager at Global Initiative for Sustainability Ratings (GISR), "the sustainability map is coming into focus". (Kaleidoscope Futures, 2015)

Specialist sustainability firms such as RobecoSAM, which manages the Dow Jones Sustainability Index, covering 59 industries and hundreds of companies, have evolved to reflect the increasing complexity of the ratings game. "The maintenance of a rating methodology, being able to identify key issues on a yearly basis, and engaging with all these companies," notes Sustainability Operations Manager, Manjit Jus, "really is a significant undertaking" (Kaleidoscope Futures, 2015).

Michael Sadowski, Director at think-tank advisory firm SustainAbility, believes that raters need to be valuable and focus on the right issues for companies. Ratings that try to deliver information to everyone will fail. "The tighter the audience," he concludes, "the more likely they will be to succeed" (Kaleidoscope Futures, 2015). Quality is also of the upmost importance, yet too many ratings have not invested in quality systems, processes and outputs to date.

As the market for sustainability information evolves, so too has confusion as to roles and interrelationships among various players across the ratings value chain. However, working together, the data disclosers, assurers, aggregators, analysts, raters and users can create positive feedback loops—a change in any one component sends ripple effects to other components through the creation of a virtuous circle of learning and innovation and synergy.

The proliferation of ratings offers investors and other stakeholders a rich pool of sustainability information and performance assessment. But this has also come at a cost. Users of ratings—particularly capital markets, but also consumers, employees, communities and others—are hard pressed to discern which ratings merit their attention and meet their decision-making needs.

Therefore, standardization, comparability and consistency are urgently required. Currently, no generally accepted methodology for this alignment has emerged, but the Global Initiative for Sustainability Ratings (GISR) is trying to respond this challenge.

Consolidation of sustainability ratings agencies

Antoine Mach, Co-Founder of Covalence, believes that "the growth and diversification of ratings over the next years will ultimately be followed by the market settling on a few 'winners' of different rating types, based on quality, due to demand" (Kaleidoscope Futures, 2015).

Elena Avesani, Product and Sustainability Manager at Oracle, believes this is happening already: "We see an increasing proliferation of sustainability ratings systems, but also a consolidation in terms of common international standards driven by the adoption from regulators and by Governments over the long term" (Kaleidoscope Futures, 2015).

This is not surprising. As demand increases for business to provide a variety of ESG related information to different rating agencies—from ethical fund managers and sustainability indexes to sustainability awards institutions and activist organizations—large, listed companies are suffering from questionnaire fatigue. This is made more acute by the lack of indicator standardization and the proliferation of would-be data users.

According to the Six Growing Trends in Corporate Sustainability report by EY (2013), some large companies respond to more than 300 customer surveys each year and the number of sustainability-related inquiries from investors and shareholders continue to increase.

The likely consequence is that companies will start to push back or simply ignore requests from all but a few ratings agencies that they judge to be the most important or influential. As a result, we expect to see a consolidation of traditional sustainability rating agencies, much like financial rating came to be dominated by the likes of Standard & Poor's, Moody's and Fitch Group.

Socially Responsible Investment (SRI) adviser, Steve Pyne, thinks:

> we need to get to a point where there are two or three renowned places with sources that can be trusted. This needs to be accessible too. It's too easy at the moment for large companies not to worry because the mainstream public don't have enough information or rating systems which individual consumers and investors can both turn to for clear information (Kaleidoscope Futures, 2015).

However, according to Darby Hobbs, CEO of Social Media 3, "it could be eight years or more before the market begins to settle, as many agencies have invested heavily in their respective methodologies". Mark Tulay, Program Manager at Global Initiative for Sustainability Ratings (GISR), is a little more bullish. He believes that, "when we get perspective, we'll see it's a renaissance period in terms of innovation and interest, in transition from viewing sustainability factors as 'value' versus 'values' based". (Kaleidoscope Futures, 2015)

Demand for more transparency by rating agencies

According to the 2014 Edelman Trust Barometer, only one in four of the general public trust business leaders to correct issues and even fewer—one in five—to tell the truth and make ethical and moral decisions.

Two thirds of the 1,000 CEOs surveyed felt business is not doing enough to address global sustainability challenges, which is one likely reason why there is a trust deficit. Good performance on independent sustainability ratings is one way to counter these low levels of trust.

However, it also leads stakeholders to question how the raters produce their ratings. Unfortunately, as commercial entities, many of these rating agencies regard their assessment methodologies as competitively sensitive intellectual property. Most raters develop and maintain proprietary methodologies in order to protect commercial interests.

Eric Whan, Director of GlobeScan's sustainability practice, calls this proprietary approach to rating methods a "black box technique", which "is not going to be very sustainable in the long term, due to the lower credibility and the fact they don't provide an avenue to trust" (Kaleidoscope Futures, 2015).

Allen White (2012), Vice President and Senior Fellow at Tellus Institute, has stressed that this gap is problematic in different ways for different users: for investors that regularly engage companies in efforts to elevate their ESG performance, opacity is a serious obstacle to efficient and effective dialogue. For corporate directors, widely variable scores impair the execution of fiduciary duties to oversee the firm's strategy and performance. For governments that might use ratings as a basis for procurement decisions, incomplete information is an obstacle to designing policies geared to screening companies on performance in areas such as human rights and climate.

As a result, demand for rating transparency is becoming stronger. When ratings are transparent across a variety of facets—their methodologies, their results, how they manage potential conflicts of interest—they build trust and stimulate demand for their products. Generally, trust in ratings is up from 2010 to 2013, although NGOs dipped slightly, while trust in investors and analysts has increased (SustainAbility, 2013).

The latest survey of "which rater is best" shows that specific ratings, such as the Carbon Disclosure Project (CDP), rank top, closely followed by the Dow Jones Sustainability Index (SustainAbility, 2013). NGOs fair especially well as raters, but there are demands for more transparency with how their rating results are achieved.

Among the traits considered most important when choosing raters, according to SustainAbility's (2013) research, are: profile, credibility, transparency of methodology and results, management buy-in or recognition of the rating (or the brand behind the rating), quality of approach and methodology and relevance of approach and criteria to a company's sector and context.

Beyond rater transparency, the challenges of inconsistency and integrity are both critical. It is suggested that many ratings methodologies rely heavily on backward-looking indicators (measuring last year's performance), as opposed to what will happen in the future over the long term. When ratings over-rely on past performance and underrepresent indicators that predict future company performance, investors and other users are left with a deficit on insight as critical questions remain unanswered.

5
Unlocking change through stakeholder engagement

Moving social media beyond a marketing channel

Of course, sustainability reports and ratings are not the only communication channel for business. Many companies today use social media—Facebook, LinkedIn, Twitter, Google+ and many others—as a "broadcast" outlet for building their brand and conveying messages to interested parties, typically those that "Like" or "Follow" them.

According to The Future of Stakeholder Engagement report by Brunswick (2013), when business experts were asked in 2013 what will be important in five years' time: 73% said monitoring social media channels; 60% noted mapping online influencers; and 46% thought creating online panels to share information.

However, Bill Baue, Co-Founder of Sustainability Context Group, believes the Accountability 1.0 mode of one-way proclamations, campaigns and PR communications on Web 2.0 platforms is already outdated. Instead, Accountability 2.0 requires two-way communication, co-operation and mutual engagement with stakeholders (Baue and Murninghan, 2010).

One first step is for companies to analyse content on social media platforms—such as the so-called Twittersphere or blogosphere—to find out the unsolicited opinions of their stakeholders. Fractal analytics, for example, uses patented technology to determine what stakeholders are saying on social media about a company's social, environmental and product performance.

However, this analytical approach is just the start. Organizations are also tapping into "crowdsourcing" and "crowdstorming" processes. Even here though, much of the crowdsourcing applied to date has been as a marketing tool: adopting Web 2.0 technologies to extend existing modes of brand communication and customer engagement. In fact, 53% of corporations are now using social media in this way, to augment their reputation preservation and crisis communication function (Useful Social Media, 2013).

Matthew Yeomans, Founder and Editor of Sustainly, believes "crowdsourcing needs to be saved from becoming a stale marketing tactic, and instead embedded into the working DNA of the company, so that it can change and influence the whole organisation" (Kaleidoscope Futures, 2015).

The real power of crowdsourcing should come from the volume of information, ideas and opinions it opens up. In addition, just as the value of user-generated content becomes more effective when curated and packaged by professional editors, crowdsourced ideas and actions increase in effectiveness when shaped around an identifiable business goal.

Engagement is already happening and it will become far more interactive. Some organizations will continue to have more robust conversations with their stakeholders online. Looking to the future, stakeholder interaction will be driven by the pressures of pluralism, the importance of continuous and frequent communications and the need for information on demand.

In a sense, the playing field has been levelled, giving stakeholders the opportunity to initiate and drive the conversation, which in turn will drive greater openness. Companies that previously demanded full control over communications now have to play by entirely different (and contradictory) rules of the game. According to the Sustainability Reporting at a Cross Roads report by Utopies (2012), nine out of ten experts expect public criticism through online social media to increase in importance over the next three to five years.

Think-tank consultancy, SustainAbility (2011b), observes that: "Companies need to get comfortable losing some control and allow conversations to evolve unedited, and some companies will benefit from unfiltered commentary and feedback from advocates and critics. Honesty, transparency and candour are even more critical online."

The new social technologies, media and networks promise—or threaten, depending on your viewpoint—to transform the reporting landscape: they will accelerate and deepen conversations between business and its current stakeholders, and, potentially, bring totally new people and interests into the conversation—with dramatically powerful information and intelligence at their disposal. Broadcast is out; dialogue in.

Kevin Petrie, Chief Procurement Officer for Nestlé in North America, reminds us that, "in the digital world, everyone has a smartphone and they want to know where things come from and share that information" (Strom, 2014).

This represents a promising approach as it has the potential to elevate sustainability reporting from a rather managerial "closed-shop" and one-way company-controlled exercise to a more stakeholder-driven process providing a variety of mechanisms for dialogue, feedback, interactivity and customization.

One interesting case in this area is the My Starbucks Idea website, where Starbucks does its business crowdsourcing. It has been actively engaging customers for years by encouraging them to submit ideas for better products, improving the customer experience, and defining new community involvement, among other categories. The company regularly polls its customers for their favourite products and has a leader board to track which customers are the most active in submitting ideas, comments, and poll participation. The site is a crowdsourcing tool, a market research method that brings customer priorities to light, an online community and an effective Internet marketing tool.

"My Starbucks Idea, though hardly a perfect model of crowdsourced action," observes Matthew Yeomans (2013), "points to what is possible in terms of better business when companies open up about the challenges they face and seek advice from parts of the community they would never have thought to consult in the past. It demonstrated some success but also had to counter criticism that their crowdsourced idea platforms are hampered by inaction."

Growing use of crowdsourcing as a stakeholder engagement tool

According to the Crowdsourcing and Social Media report by Weber Shandwick/KRC Research (2010), 44% of corporate sustainability mangers say they have used crowdsourcing to help in decision-making on how to tackle issues, 83% see the potential in crowdsourcing technology and 95% "found it valuable to their company".

Crowdsourcing—which emerged from thinking on the "wisdom of the crowd" and "wikinomics"—is made possible due to Web 2.0 technologies, which allow participation and aggregation of the views of large numbers of people. While there are celebrated examples such as Open Planet Ideas and FutureScapes, where crowdsourcing is used to create innovation ("crowd-storming"), it has attracted the most interest as a stakeholder engagement tool.

According to The Future of Stakeholder Engagement report by Brunswick (2013), four in five communicators (82%) believe their organization will be doing more stakeholder engagement in five years' time, and crowdsourcing may be the perfect tool to respond to that demand.

Crowdsourcing creates networks that enable people to act together in new ways and in situations where collective action was not possible before. It is likely that the "killer apps" of tomorrow's mobile infocom industry will not be hardware devices or software programmes but online infrastructures that facilitate relationships among enterprises, communities and markets.

Sustainability managers believe the value of crowdsourcing is that it surfaces new perspectives, builds engagement with key audiences, invites clients and customers from nontraditional sources to contribute ideas and brings new energy to the process of generating ideas and content.

These benefits have become especially evident when companies can select an "expert crowd" to engage with, as new platforms such as Convetit allow. Hence, organizations an tap into the crowdsourcing or crowdstorming process selectively, as a complement to existing business practices.

Explaining how it works, Thomas O'Malley, Founder and CEO of Convetit, says: "I can press the button and I'm going to be launched into a think tank of some sorts with these ten people who've already been pre-vetted. And we are going to engage for a short period of time to solve my problem" (Kaleidoscope Futures, 2015).

Unilever is one of the companies that have been experimenting with crowdsourcing. In April 2012, Unilever launched its first ever Sustainable Living Lab—a 24-hour continuous discussion to bring together different stakeholders from around the world to address some of the most difficult challenges faced in the journey towards sustainable growth, including sustainable sourcing, sustainable production and distribution, consumer behaviour change, and waste and recycling. More than 2,200 participants from 77 countries took part in the Sustainability Lab forums to discuss ideas, develop solutions and share good practice in four key areas of the value chain. Almost 4,000 comments were posted during the Lab and one year later, the exercise was repeated.

In 2013, a separate campaign, Project Sunlight, was launched, which was an ambitious effort to raise consumer awareness about sustainability through the company's leading brands. It's too early to say just how success-ful Project Sunlight will be in educating and shaping consumer behaviour, but the pure scale of Unilever's focus on sustainability marketing—and the potential of social media to ignite a movement—will make more than a few other chief marketing officers sit up and take note.

Transforming the power of connection into the power of collaboration

Many companies have used Web 2.0 as a means of communicating, understanding their stakeholder needs and responding to their concerns. However, the real power of crowdsourcing type technologies is not in con-sultation but in collaboration—when groups of people who share a com-mon vision can link together to make change happen.

"For crowdsourcing to be an effective part of social business, the 'crowd' needs to feel that its views (so assiduously courted by the corporation) turn into action," says Matthew Yeomans (2013).

Online collaboration can take many forms. For example, BlaBlaCar con-nects drivers with empty seats to people looking for a ride and is the biggest European car sharing community. Karmayog in India allows the public to blow the whistle on bribery and collectively put pressure on government officials to stamp out corruption. Things.info pools information about the production, usage and recycling of products to improve our social and envi-ronmental footprint.

By far the most popular form of online collaboration, however, is via social media. The 2013 Sustainability Social Media Index (Sustainly, 2013). reports that nearly half of the 475 global, publicly listed companies they analysed have social media channels or campaigns dedicated to discussing their sus-tainability or CSR efforts. Just four years ago only 60 major companies were using social media for sustainability.

Twitter is the most popular (and easiest to handle) social media chan-nel for most companies. Increasingly companies are also experimenting with Pinterest, Tumblr and Instagram for storytelling, as well as looking to

LinkedIn to provide thought leadership. Apps and interactive games also provide useful content outlets and create a more interesting experience around sustainability and CSR topics.

Although internal, crowdlike approaches to creativity and idea generation—such as "jams", "idea marketplaces" and "personal entrepreneurial projects"—may increase the scope for exploration and flexibility inside companies, they are qualitatively different from and fall short of the full capability of external crowds.

By contrast, Buycott is an example where crowdsourcing is used as a collaborative, action-oriented tool. Buycott enables consumers to scan bar codes on packaging to uncover details of the product's corporate family tree and allows consumers to join user-created campaigns to boycott businesses that support questionable practices. It is possible to consumers to join user-created campaigns, which include a list of companies to avoid or support in order to achieve a goal. When a person scans a product barcode, the app traces the ownership of that product to its top corporate parent and cross-checks it against the campaign commitments a person has made.

Founder, Ivan Pardo, states: "For me, it was critical to allow users to create campaigns because I don't think it's Buycott's role to tell people what to buy. We simply want to provide a platform that empowers consumers to make well-informed purchasing decisions" (O'Connor, 2013).

Hyper-connectivity makes responsiveness more possible

In the coming decade, 2.5–3 billion more users could be connected to the Internet. Most of this growth will occur in developing economies. The rapid growth of social media (and user-generated content) will undoubtedly continue apace, to the extent that, by 2025, more than 1.8 billion people will move up into the global consumer class. The leading agent for connecting these billions of consumers will be mobile-computing devices, particularly smartphones. (McKinsey, 2013)

As our technologies make hyper-connectivity the norm rather than the exception, we all have the potential to be citizen activists. We can "vote" using social media to make our opinions heard instantly through Twitter or Facebook or any of the other online platforms. But the ubiquity of online networks also means that we are overwhelmed by content and flooded with requests to participate in everything from games and surveys to webinars and think-tanks. As a result, we screen out or ignore many invitations to engage.

Technology alone does not create constructive engagement and collaboration. Awareness and participation invariably count enormously. Each day millions of blog postings are written and hundreds of thousands of videos are uploaded onto YouTube, to be shared, "Liked" and commented on. Twitter has over half a billion accounts and over 200 million tweets a day. Communications experts Jon Miller and Lucy Parker describe this as the "age of conversation" (Miller and Parker, 2013).

Perhaps the best example of collaborative conversations is the Wikipedia model. Wikis grow because enough people care about them; they die if the converse is true. The chief challenge facing intermediaries that have created online stakeholder engagement platforms, therefore, is getting people to show up, beyond the initial novelty phase. After this, it is even harder to promote continuous participation.

Charles Arthur (2006) from *The Guardian* points out that, "in Internet culture, the 1% rule is a rule of thumb pertaining to participation in an Internet community, stating that only 1% of the users of a website actively create new content, while the other 99% of the participants just lurk". A variant is the 90–9–1 principle (sometimes also presented as the 89:10:1 ratio), which states that in a collaborative website such as a wiki, 90% of the participants of a community only view content, 9% of the participants edit content and 1% of the participants actively create new content.

Despite these challenges to engagement, according to the Re:Thinking Consumption report by BBMG, Globescan and SustainAbility (2012), two thirds of consumers globally (67%) are interested in sharing their ideas, opinions and experiences with companies to help them develop better products or create new solutions.

Of course, if contributions are undervalued or there are limited incentives, then interest will waver and participation will suffer, resulting in fewer contributions and ultimately disengagement from the platform.

Value–action gaps make stakeholder feedback less valuable

Social media allows companies to communicate more widely and subtly with potential customers about the values associated with their products and services, especially its ethical, socially responsible or environmentally sustainable attributes.

However, Web 2.0 type technologies have exacerbated the value–action gap, whereby people's expressed attitudes or values—which are easier and less costly than ever to share—are not matched by their actions, such as, altered buying behaviour. We sometimes also call this "slacktivism".

It has been suggested by Internet expert, Evgeny Morozov (2009), that increased online presence has done little more than create a generation of "slacktivists" who will engage in token displays of support for a cause but are not likely to subsequently engage in more meaningful contributions to the cause. While this may be true in some instances, there is no doubt that significant movements have been driven through the Internet to affect important change. One example is www.change.org, which is a web-based technology tool with a transparent action agenda.

In fact, crowdsourcing is a fertile ground for grass-roots activists to campaign on causes. Transparency expert, Bill Baue, however, is sceptical about self-organized action. "If you don't have any sense of guidance or a mechanism for discerning the actions from the aggregation of data, then it's merely a dumping ground that doesn't have assessment or analysis or a logical next step." Baue advises that companies must "avoid the 'if you build it they will come' mentality; rather it's better to leave a trail of breadcrumbs to the tools on how to use it to create change dynamics. That's where the innovation of crowds is great" (Kaleidoscope Futures, 2015).

Companies are obviously directly engaged in social media activities on a continuous basis. But businesses need skilled facilitators and moderators who are well versed in constructing online collaborative communities to effectively manage their external relations. Typically, this involves managing a complex set of tasks, including facilitating discourse, connecting and applying new ideas, focusing the discussion, correcting misconceptions, distinguishing between facts and opinions, and managing conflicts.

Important questions to pose are: What is the added value for a corporation to participate? How deep can these conversations go? And what are the risks associated with public positioning on specific issues through these channels?

The wisdom of the crowd can become the tragedy of the commons

Crowdsourcing allows everyone to express his or her opinion, promoting diversity of feedback. It can foster the emergence of collective knowledge and the revelation of formerly invisible insights. Good or popular ideas can rise to the top.

However, in terms of stakeholder theory, *who* says something can be even more important than *what* they say. For opinions to be credible, therefore, the source of those opinions needs to be trusted. Hence, validation, vetting and referencing is critical. If no one accepts constraints or rules, the "tragedy of the commons" may result.

The veracity of any claim made against a business is crucial. In terms of allegations put forward by NGOs, corporate rating agencies sometimes have to dismiss information advanced to them due to the credibility of the information and source provided. Businesses in turn have concerns that claims may be biased, incomplete, or politically motivated. Furthermore, there are invariably risks related to superficial assessments based on only limited information, such as what has been reported in the media.

As noted before, one of the primary concerns related to existing rating systems is the lack of traceability. It is therefore necessary to pay close attention to the source and be very explicit, so the end-user knows. "Trust is the biggest factor—you can't have points of fail," concludes Alexander Gillett, CEO of How Good (Kaleidoscope Futures, 2015).

The experiences of Wikipedia and other projects that rely on user-generated content demonstrate that a combination of detailed guidelines and active communities can eliminate a lot of inaccurate content. Notwithstanding these controls, public platforms do invite distorted representations from both corporate sources and overzealous consumer activists.

There are fears that corporations can game any system with their large resources and PR teams, thus allowing them to be unfairly rewarded within a rating system. On the other hand, businesses note how NGOs use platforms to lobby, for whistle-blowing and to further their interests by making a series of claims against companies. And then when companies are not responsive to demands, activists use the Internet to pepper management with detailed inquiries.

These outcomes can lead to a modern version of "the tragedy of the commons", where each individual maximizing their own benefit leads to a negative collective outcome. For instance, many would agree that a fair playing field with some individual constraints is good for a healthy stakeholder dialogue. Yet the incentives and behaviour of the individual contributors may work against that outcome. "It's really tricky to avoid simply sliding into a place where mud gets slung," admits Caroline Rees, President of Shift (Kaleidoscope Futures, 2015).

The openness of open source is questionable

The biggest strength of open source platforms is their openness. The bigger the crowd, the more diverse the opinions, the better. By using crowdsourcing as a form of watchdog or rating system, companies can feel real pressure to improve their performance.

However, as soon as sustainability criteria are introduced to a collaborative platform, the crowd is self-selecting. Hence, it is not a truly representative forum for opinions. Besides this, interpretation of value-laden concepts such as social, ethical and environmental performance may add confusion rather than clarity.

Consumers and stakeholders have very different concerns. They also come with different agendas. There are facts and there are interpretations of facts. NGOs and businesses may likely disagree; and perhaps that tension may simply be unresolvable. Perspective is everything.

"A lot of sustainability information is qualitative," admits Jules Peck, Founder of Jericho Chambers. "It's very subjective in terms what's good, bad, and different. It's also pretty hard to compare" (Kaleidoscope Futures, 2015).

For the most part, consumers and stakeholders have very different sets of concerns. Any weighting system that is constructed will not satisfy everybody. "Values based ratings are very different—and materially so—from 'value' based ratings. Often we co-mingle the two," explains Mark Tulay, Program Manager at Global Initiative for Sustainability Ratings (GISR).

One organization that has had to deal with values-based content is the BASEwiki (Business and Society Engaging for Solutions) project, a Web 2.0 platform for information exchange and learning in the human rights space. It is a relatively small-scale wiki with well-informed stakeholders. When asked for feedback, the majority of the stakeholders emphasized the need for "the site to have more centrally curated information due to the risks associated with quality control".

There is also a danger that unsubstantiated or false claims made on open source platforms could derail a constructive stakeholder dialogue that is already ongoing. In some instances, this could easily impede progress. A further repercussion is for different agendas to be introduced as a result of the participatory focus (because civil society groups are hugely disparate), which could affect ongoing discussions negatively.

"The essence of a Wiki platform is that you don't censor," explains Darby Hobbs, CEO of Social 3. "But companies have their compliance officers; and given how firms are regulated in the US, I'm not sure how much flexibility there will be for them to engage" (Kaleidoscope Futures, 2015).

Not surprisingly, corporations are highly sensitive to any allegations put forward, whether substantiated or not. A truly open forum for opinions inevitably brings with it questions of legal liability, especially in the litigious United States.

Steve Lydenberg, Chief Investment Officer at Domini Social Investments, observes that, in America, "everything tends to be very carefully vetted by Counsel; and any public dialogue will involve companies corresponding statements to their public corporate responsibility reports—it will be a slow back and forth" (Kaleidoscope Futures, 2015).

Questions remain about ratings when the guardians are not guarded

Accountability ratings have the potential for encouraging greater organizational transparency, especially on sustainability performance. By putting companies and issues in the spotlight, it also encourages them to be more accountable for their actions.

However, every rating system is subjective—run by an institution and individuals with their own values and agenda. The methodologies use screening criteria for inclusion of content and rules for assigning scores to performance. How transparent are these processes, and who checks the consistency or fairness of the raters?

A core characteristic of any rating system—be it wiki-based, or created by experts—is that they end up presenting one view of the truth. Undoubted, there is debate that happens in the background, but this is ultimately hidden from the public, in favour of simplicity and readability. The values or biases inherent in those debates is also hidden from view. So who is checking behind the curtain? Who is guarding the guardians?

The well-respected Business and Human Rights Centre has been held up as a beacon of good (if imperfect) practice: whenever it receives an allegation, it goes out to the companies involved and asks for their comments; and likewise, they go to NGOs when businesses issue positive PR. Caroline Rees suggests this is like "a half-way house, which allows information to be shared, but also the chance to respond". Even so, concerns remain. Rees wonders: "Is it is possible to avoid becoming an online court of arbitration that passes judgment, or instead let allegations pass?" (Kaleidoscope Futures, 2015).

The Ethical Consumer Research Association (ECRA) tries to mitigate against potential bias problems by extensive training of their researchers on how to vet and upload sustainability-related information to its database. There is also a system of verification required by senior researchers.

Most acknowledge that it is incredibly difficult to vet information that comes in from users. Even for experts, it's challenging to understand what the real story is. Even so, Pratap Chatterjee, Executive Director of CorpWatch, is adamant that "an open source model is not necessarily a great model if not monitored by a third party" (Kaleidoscope Futures, 2015).

We constantly need to ask: How transparent are these vetting processes, and who checks the consistency or fairness of the raters?

In search of the Web 2.0-savvy players

The past few years has seen a boom in the creation of Web 2.0-savvy platforms and ratings that empower customers and communities with knowledge about the social, environmental and ethical impacts of the products and the companies that produce them. In fact, 2014 was described as "the tipping point for enterprise collaboration" and some predict more crowd-based information will arise from various sources. Here are signposts to some favourites.

- **Convetit** is a platform that makes it easy for passionate professionals to tackle sustainability challenges in a collaborative virtual environment.

- **Ethiscore.org** is designed to rank companies based on a range of criteria that can be customized to each person's ethical, political and environmental preferences.

- **Good Guide** is in business to provide authoritative information about the health, environmental and social performance of products and companies. Its mission is to help consumers make purchasing decisions that reflect their preferences and values.

- **Global Forest Watch (GFW)** is an interactive website that improves transparency and accountability in forest management decisions by increasing the public's access to information on forestry developments around the World.

- **Howstuffismade.org** is a visual encyclopedia of the production processes of everyday goods.

- **Knowmore** is a grass-roots, web-based community dedicated to chronicling and resisting corporate attacks on democracy, workers' and human rights, fair trade, business ethics and the environment, with a shared goal of a more informed and conscious consumer.

- **Star Communities** is a voluntary, self-reporting framework for evaluating, quantifying and improving the liveability and sustainability of US communities.

- **Supplyshift** is a cloud-based sustainability management platform designed to help companies engage with their suppliers and use sustainability information to improve supply chain performance and reduce risk.

- **Wikipositive** was set up to provide a free, open-access collaborative platform designed to be a simple starting point for social and environmental research.

- **Wikirate** is a community-driven initiative designed to "make companies clear" by providing an open platform for corporate transparency. The information is created by and for anyone who interacts with companies, including consumers, employees, investors, management and regulators.

Convetit keeps our head in the cloud and feet on the ground

As you can see, an unprecedented number of collaborative initiatives have developed in recent years among corporations and NGOs, suppliers, employees, and consumers. Even so, basic logistical barriers limit the practice. To achieve scale, engagement must be easier and less burdensome to the scarce resources of sustainability and strategy offices. Fortunately, technology solutions are rising to meet this need.

One company, Convetit, has developed a platform that makes it easy for passionate professionals to tackle sustainability challenges in a collaborative virtual environment. The site provides an all-in-one outlet to identify individuals, engage them in week-long focus groups through text, video, and surveys, and publish resulting insights in highly visual summaries. The outcome: a faster, more affordable, less carbon-intensive way of harvesting and distilling professional, action-oriented solutions to problems that matter.

But with the amount of noise in busy professionals' lives, does online engagement work? "Given the number of issues that require collaborative response to realize a sustainable future, the question is not *can it work* but *how can it work best*?" insists Convetit CEO Tom O'Malley. His team has designed the platform based on leading research from Harvard and Cambridge to ensure the proper incentives and motivation for participation. Some think-tanks include $100 in-kind donations to charity for participants to share their insights, for example, to ensure a sense of shared accountability for outcomes. "It's an iterative process, but we are learning quickly and implementing improvements every day," says O'Malley. (Kaleidoscope Futures, 2015)

So far, the applications are impressive. Private conversations have been conducted to vet sustainability reports among key stakeholders, make more inclusive and transparent investment decisions, and surface best practices for human rights standards among supplier communities. Public dialogues have enabled companies to advance important social and environmental discourse and respond to public challenges with enhanced speed. To counter misinformation around how to contain the Ebola epidemic, for example, one organization sponsored a week-long discussion among experts in infectious disease, public policy, epidemiology, and emergency response in late 2014. The five-day conversation resulted in a suggested plan of action for hospital networks operating in the US—a process that otherwise would have taken weeks of co-ordination.

What makes Convetit's model perhaps most interesting and potentially disruptive is its migration of sharing economy principles to the professional arena. Operating as a platform provider only, the company's success directly correlates with the success of an ecosystem of partners who are accessing new professional opportunities by bringing their services to the platform: consultants, facilitators, expert networks, writers and designers. The model is providing an outlet for freelancers and making traditional service providers more relevant, interesting and responsive to their clients.

Living well within our collective means requires new ways of doing things. For its ability to bring together people, ideas and services in direct response to the sustainability imperatives we face, Convetit is an interesting example of a company leading the way.

Wikirate strives to make companies clear

Let's look at another platform, Wikirate, in a bit more detail to see how this landscape is shaping up. Wikirate is an independent, neutral, not-for-profit open community with a vision of driving deep corporate transparency so citizens can steer companies to create a better world. Platform participants work together to create informative, reliable profiles on companies' social and environmental performance. This comprises the "wiki" part of Wikirate. In 2015, as part of their beta release, they will also introduce metrics, the "rate" part of Wikirate.

In 2016, they also plan to roll out Wikirate 1.0, which will feature many more tools for calculating, standardizing, scoring, and visualizing ratings, multilingual support, and a host of other improvements. Wikirate 1.0 will make it possible for sustainability data to be more abundant, organized, presentable, and usable than ever before.

It aims to make ratings transparent, by allowing users to review and challenge every part of the process. It will also make ratings scalable, by allowing communities and organizations to collaborate on populating the data on which the ratings are based. It will make ratings dynamic, by allowing people to re-use data to create new ratings. Further, metric designers will be rewarded for creating metrics that Wikirate users consider important, and it will reward companies for transparently providing data for those metrics.

Furthermore, Wikirate 1.0 is still just a first phase, in which companies are still largely measured individually. The vision of Wikirate 2.0 is to measure companies as part of a network. How will Wikirate do it?

Today it is already possible to explore and contribute to the "wiki" element of Wikirate. On the numerous company pages, there are lots of articles organized into social and environmental topics. These are community-edited, like most wikis, but Wikirate offers additional tools to make sure the articles are trustworthy and well sourced. Articles must cite claims, which are short, simple sourced statements about companies. The community openly discusses and votes on claims to determine their importance. The most important claims receive the greatest emphasis.

According to Philipp Hirche, Founder of Wikirate:

> Wikirate is set up to fundamentally change the world of CSR ratings. Its 100% transparency, maximum potential for stakeholder involvement, its independence, its not-for-profit status and its innovative open-source data platform are all key ingredients to better ratings. But above all, Wikirate wants to assure a fair dialogue. We are not here to scold companies, but to engage stakeholders to help companies become better corporate citizens. (Kaleidoscope Futures, 2015)

Then the "rate" element of Wikirate comes online, the public will be able to compare companies directly using hundreds of different metrics. Just as with claims, users will be able to choose which metrics they would like to appear most prominently throughout the site. Community members of the site will be able to help contribute research on these metrics and even add their own.

Wikirate's ratings framework is designed to engage advocacy groups, company representatives and individuals as respected contributors. Companies are rewarded for transparency, advocacy groups are rewarded for creating important metrics and individuals can contribute to every aspect of the site. Wikirate isn't on a mission to name and shame; rather, it strives to use transparency to promote responsibility. A fair dialogue is at the core of their mission.

According to Hirche, what makes Wikirate so special compared with other rating providers is that it embraces the following core concepts:

- **Full transparency on all levels**: at Wikirate, there is 100% transparency on data and methodology. Even data that is not used in a rating is being made available.

- **Potential for maximum stakeholder involvement**: any advocacy group can use Wikirate as a platform for their rating. There will thus be many different ratings focusing on different areas and with different levels of breath and depth on Wikirate. By starting a rating on Wikirate, advocacy groups can engage with their members, subscribers or volunteers to create, populate and disseminate a rating together. Companies will be encouraged to create a profile on Wikirate and participate in the dialogue.

- **Changing the question/answer game**: anyone will be able to post questions to companies on Wikirate regarding their CSR efforts. The model where many different rating providers ask the same questions to companies and the company responds separately is outdated. Any question and answer should be made public, and Wikirate aims to be the place to post questions and answers.

- **Effective communication of the quality of content**: the full transparency of Wikirate, combined with its voting system, allows appropriate filtering for and communication of the quality of content on Wikirate, a key prerequisite for building trust. There will be areas of excellence, likely where advocacy groups shepherd the rating process, and there will be areas where more time and community effort is needed to get to quality content.

- **Independence**: Wikirate is set up as a nonprofit entity, relying on grants and donations by its members. We do not have conflicts of interests other commercial rating providers may have. Also, Wikirate understands itself not as an advocacy organization (except perhaps for transparency) but rather sees its main task to assure fairness in the dialogue and ratings on Wikirate.

- **Vast extension potential**: Wikirate's open data structure allows extensions to Wikirate to, for example, enable suppliers to self-report CSR information, or to collect feedback from affected employees or communities, and integrate this information in company ratings. This innovation will be captured in the future Wikirate 2.0.

Business accountability in a fish-bowl future

To conclude this chapter, it is clear that business will increasingly live in a "fish-bowl" world of transparency and stakeholder engagement. The last few years have seen a major shift in the way in which stakeholders are being used as a materiality filter for reporting on the most critical, impactful performance indicators. As the reporting becomes more focused, so does the depth of analysis and presentation. At the same time, quantification is moving gradually towards financial costing and disclosure of social and environmental externalities. Companies are realizing that *context* and *impact* are today's reporting watchwords.

Another change is that the one-size-fits-all, half narrative, half quantified sustainability report is looking increasingly out of date. Instead, companies are expected to draw on their growing database of environmental, social and governance (ESG) information and tailor it to different audiences. Performance data now needs to be packaged in different formats, with different stories, using different communications channels and media, in order to match the diversity of stakeholders' expectations.

Linked to this trend is the localization and customizability of reports. Readers are only interested in what is directly relevant to them, so they will increasingly need to be able to interact with disclosed ESG content and shape it into a format that suits their needs and answers their specific questions.

We have seen that ratings are becoming more important, more numerous and more mainstream. There is also increasing demand for greater transparency in this arena, which is unsurprising: good performance on independent sustainability ratings is one way that businesses can counter the low levels of trust felt by the public at large.

But now business has a new trust arena to play in. Ever since Yochai Benkler's *The Wealth of Networks* (Benkler, 2006) and Dan Tapscott and Anthony D. Williams' *Wikinomics* (Tapscott and Williams, 2007), business has been getting to grips with how the user-generated content world of Web 2.0 is reshaping what they do and how. For stakeholders, the social media revolution brings the democratization of information on companies that was previously the preserve of a much smaller set of infomediaries.

The stakeholders' dream, according to the Volans and GRI (2010) Transparent Economy report, is "a comprehensive, networked, real time, platform that provided a single version of the truth to all concerned parties, inside and out". The crowdsourcing models that have emerged in response are one of the ways stakeholders are taking collaborative communications into their own hands. In effect, hyper-connectivity is allowing everyone to become a citizen activist, using the wisdom of the crowd to regulate corporate behaviour.

What this means for business is that companies will increasingly face connected citizens that are checking compliance to regulations and codes, organizing public campaigns than name and shame offenders and changing customer's buying behaviour. This trend builds on steady improvements in consumer information on sustainable products and companies, which is coming out of the ratings revolution.

However, companies can also turn the social media revolution to their advantage, by engaging in tailored crowdsourcing with stakeholders and sustainability experts. They need to ensure that these groups are properly represented, as many wiki-type platforms still exclude marginalized communities and those from less developed countries. However, if done thoughtfully, crowd-based platforms, linked to information on supply chains, products and corporate performance, could empower stakeholders around the world to help companies innovate to become more sustainable and responsible.

6
Unlocking change through social responsibility

The rise and fall of CSR

Perhaps a more direct way to unlock change on the path to more sustainable frontiers is through corporate social responsibility (CSR). Or is it? Those who have read my previous books, notably *The Age of Responsibility* (Visser, 2011) and *CSR 2.0* (Visser, 2013), will be already be familiar with the basic arguments in this chapter, although you may find the addition of practical steps for application to be useful. For others, I will outline in the next few pages how CSR has changed over time, the challenges it currently faces, and what it would mean to make it a truly transformative practice.

To begin, we must acknowledge that CSR is nothing new. The concept can be traced at least as far as the mid- to late 1800s. Industrialists such as John H. Patterson of National Cash Register seeded the industrial welfare movement while philanthropists such as John D. Rockefeller set a precedent that is echoed today in the work of business titan such as Bill Gates.

CSR entered the popular lexicon in the 1950s with R. Bowen's landmark book, *Social Responsibilities of the Businessman* (Bowen, 1953). The concept was strengthened in the 1960s, with Rachel Carson's critique of the chemicals industry in *Silent Spring* (Carson, 1962) that helped to birth the environmental movement. CSR gained momentum in the consumer arena with Ralph Nader's triumph over General Motors and its unsafe automotive manufacturing processes.

By the 1990s, CSR was being institutionalized through standards such as ISO 14001 (for environmental management systems) and SA 8000 (for labour rights), as well as guidelines such as the Global Reporting Initiative and corporate governance codes such as Cadbury and King. During the 21st century, an even greater plethora of CSR guidelines, codes and standards have been spawned; there are more than 100 listed in *The A to Z of Corporate Social Responsibility* (Visser *et al.*, 2007).

Despite this steady march of progress, however, I believe CSR has broadly failed. We are in fact witnessing the decline of CSR, which will continue until its natural death, unless it is reborn and rejuvenated. While CSR has had a positive impact on both communities and the environment, its success should be judged within the context of the total impact of business on society and the planet. From this perspective, CSR has failed on virtually every measure of social, ecological and ethical performance we have available.

A few facts will suffice to make the point: our global ecological footprint has more than tripled since 1961; WWF's Living Planet Index shows a 52% species decline since 1970; and 60% of the world's ecosystems have been degraded, according to the Millennium Ecosystem Assessment (2005).

We do not fare much better on social issues: according to the UNDP (2006), one billion people in the world live on less than one dollar a day. Another 2.7 billion struggle to survive on less than two dollars per day. More than 2.6 billion people—over 40% of the world's population—do not have basic sanitation, and more than one billion people still use unsafe sources of drinking water.

There is little good news to report on ethical issues either. According to the Global Corruption Barometer 2013 across 107 countries, 27% have paid a bribe when accessing public services and institutions in the last year. Add to this the litany of corporate scandals over the last few decades, starting with Enron's collapse in fraudulent disgrace in 2001, despite *Fortune* magazine having voted it one of the "100 Best Companies to Work for in America".

What can we conclude, other than: "Houston, we have a problem!"

The ages and stages of CSR

I have found it useful to view the evolution of business responsibility in terms of five overlapping periods—the Ages of Greed, Philanthropy, Marketing, Management and Responsibility—each of which typically manifests a different stage of CSR, namely: Defensive, Charitable, Promotional, Strategic and Transformative CSR, as described in Table 1.

Economic age	Stage of CSR	Modus operandi	Key enabler	Stakeholder target
Greed	Defensive	Ad hoc interventions	Investments	Shareholders, government and employees
Philanthropy	Charitable	Charitable programmes	Projects	Communities
Marketing	Promotional	Public relations	Media	General public
Management	Strategic	Management systems	Codes	Shareholders and NGOs/CSOs
Responsibility	Transformative	Business models	Products	Regulators and customers

TABLE 1   The ages and stages of CSR

My contention is that companies tend to move through these ages and stages (although they may have activities in several ages and stages at once), and that we should be encouraging business to make the transition to Transformative CSR in the dawning Age of Responsibility. If companies remain stuck in any of the first four stages, I don't believe we will turn the tide on the environmental, social and ethical crises that we face. Simply put, CSR will continue to fail.

Let me introduce the ages and stages of CSR here briefly.

- **Defensive CSR** in the Age of Greed exists when all corporate sustainability and responsibility practices—which are typically limited—are undertaken only if and when it can be shown that shareholder value will be protected as a result. Hence, employee volunteer programmes (which show evidence of improved staff motivation, commitment and productivity) are not uncommon, nor are targeted expenditures (for example, on pollution controls), which are seen to fend off regulation or avoid fines and penalties.

- **Charitable CSR** in the Age of Philanthropy is where a company supports various social and environmental causes through donations and sponsorships, typically administered through a Foundation, Trust or Chairman's Fund and aimed at empowering community groups or civil society organizations (CSOs). We often hear companies saying their CSR is about "giving back" to society, which is a clue that they are still practising Charitable CSR.

- **Promotional CSR** in the Age of Marketing is what happens when corporate sustainability and responsibility is seen mainly as a public relations opportunity to enhance the brand, image and reputation of the company. Promotional CSR may draw on the practices of Charitable and Strategic CSR and turn them into PR spin, which is often characterized as "greenwash".

- **Strategic CSR**, emerging from the Age of Management, means relating CSR activities to the company's core business (such as Coca-Cola's focus on water management), often through adherence to CSR codes and implementation of social and environmental management systems, which typically involve cycles of CSR policy development, goal and target setting, programme implementation, auditing and reporting.

- **Transformative CSR**—or CSR 2.0—in the Age of Responsibility focuses its activities on identifying and tackling the root causes of our present unsustainability and irresponsibility, typically through innovating business models, revolutionizing their processes, products and services and lobbying for progressive national and international policies.

Hence, while Strategic CSR is focused at the micro level—supporting social or environmental issues that happen to align with its strategy (but without necessarily changing that strategy)—Transformative CSR focuses on understanding the interconnections of the macro-level system—society and ecosystems—and changing its strategy to optimize the outcomes for this larger human and ecological system.

The triple failures of CSR

Why then have the first four stages of CSR failed so spectacularly to address the very issues they claim to be most concerned about? This comes down to three factors, which I call the Triple Failures of Modern CSR.

Failure 1: Incremental CSR

One of the great revolutions of the 1970s was total quality management (TQM), conceived by American statistician W. Edwards Deming, perfected by the Japanese and exported around the world as ISO 9001. At the very core of Deming's TQM model and the ISO standard is continual improvement, a principle that has now become ubiquitous in all management system approaches to performance. The most popular environmental management standard, ISO 14001, is also built on the same principle.

There is nothing wrong with continuous improvement *per se*. On the contrary, it has brought safety and reliability to the very products and services that we associate with modern quality of life. But when we use it as the primary approach to tackling our social, environmental and ethical challenges, it fails on two critical counts: speed and scale. The incremental approach of CSR, while replete with evidence of micro-scale, gradual improvements, has completely and utterly failed to make any impact on the massive sustainability crises that we face, many of which are getting worse at a pace that far outstrips any futile CSR-led attempts at amelioration.

Failure 2: Peripheral CSR

Ask any CSR manager what their greatest frustration is and they will tell you: lack of top management commitment. This is coded language for saying that CSR is, at best, a peripheral function in most companies. There may be a CSR manager, a CSR department even, a CSR report and a public commitment to any number of CSR codes and standards. But these do little to mask the underlying truth that shareholder-driven capitalism is rampant and its obsession with short-term financial measures of progress is contradictory in almost every way to the long-term, stakeholder approach needed for high-impact CSR.

The reason Lehman Brothers collapsed, and, indeed, the reason that our current financial crisis spiralled out of control, was not rogue executives or creative accounting practices, but rather a culture of greed embedded in the DNA of the company and the financial markets. It is difficult to find many substantive examples in which the financial markets consistently reward responsible behaviour.

Failure 3: Uneconomic CSR

If there was ever a monotonously repetitive, stuck record in CSR debates, it is the need for the so-called "business case" for CSR. CSR managers and consultants (even the occasional saintly CEO) are desperate for compelling evidence that "doing good is good for business" (i.e. CSR pays). Indeed, the lack of sympathetic research is no impediment for these desperados endlessly incanting the motto of the business case, as if it were an entirely self-evident fact.

The more "inconvenient truth" is that CSR sometimes pays, in specific circumstances, but more often does not. There is low-hanging fruit—such as eco-efficiencies around waste and energy—but these only go so far. The hardcore CSR changes that are needed to reverse the misery of poverty and the sixth mass extinction of species require strategic change and massive investment. These may be lucrative in the long term, economically rational over a generation or two, but we have already established that the financial markets don't work like that; at least, not yet.

CSR 1.0 and burying the past

So CSR must be seen for what it is: an outdated, outmoded artefact that was once useful, whose time has passed. If we admit the failure of CSR, we may find ourselves on the cusp of a revolution, like the one that transformed the Internet from Web 1.0 to Web 2.0. The emergence of social media networks, user-generated content and open source approaches are a fitting metaphor for the changes CSR must undergo to redefine its contribution and make a serious impact on the social, environmental and ethical challenges that the world faces.

For example, just as the Internet of Web 1.0 moved from a passive audience, content consumption approach to a collaborative mode of Google/Facebook-type interaction, CSR 1.0 is starting to move beyond the outmoded

Web 1.0	CSR 1.0
A flat world just beginning to connect itself and finding a new medium to push out information and plug advertising.	A vehicle for companies to establish relationships with communities, channel philanthropic contributions and manage their image.
Saw the rise to prominence of innovators such as Netscape, but these were quickly out-muscled by giants such as Microsoft with its Internet Explorer.	Included many start-up pioneers such as Traidcraft, but has ultimately turned into a product for large multinationals such as Walmart.
Focused largely on the standardized hardware and software of the PC as its delivery platform, rather than multilevel applications.	Travelled down the road of "one size fits all" standardization, through codes, standards and guidelines to shape its offering.

TABLE 2   Similarities between Web 1.0 and CSR 1.0

Web 2.0	CSR 2.0
Being defined by watchwords such as "collective intelligence", "collaborative networks" and "user participation".	Being defined by "global commons", "innovative partnerships" and "stakeholder involvement".
Tools include social media, knowledge syndication and beta testing.	Mechanisms include diverse stakeholder panels, real-time transparent reporting and new-wave social entrepreneurship.
Is as much a state of being as a technical advance—it is a new philosophy or way of seeing the world differently.	Is recognizing a shift in power from centralized to decentralized; a change in scale from few and big to many and small; and a change in application from single and exclusive to multiple and shared.

TABLE 3   Similarities between Web 2.0 and CSR 2.0

approach of CSR as philanthropy or public relations (widely criticized as "greenwash") to a more interactive, stakeholder-driven model. Web 1.0 was dominated by standardized hardware and software, while Web 2.0 encourages co-creation and diversity. So too in CSR, where we are beginning to realize the limitations of the generic CSR codes and standards that have proliferated in the past ten years. The similarities between Web 1.0 and CSR 1.0 are illustrated in Table 2.

If this is where we have come from, where do we need to go to? The similarities between Web 2.0 and CSR 2.0 are illustrated in Table 3.

Let us explore in more detail this revolution that will, if successful, change the way we talk about and practise CSR and, ultimately, the way we do business. There are five principles that make up the DNA of CSR 2.0: creativity, scalability, responsiveness, glocality and circularity.

The principle of creativity in CSR 2.0

In order to succeed in the CSR revolution, we will need innovation and creativity. We know from Thomas Kuhn's work on *The Structure of Scientific Revolutions* (Kuhn, 1962) that step-change only happens when we can re-perceive our world, when we can find a genuinely new paradigm, or pattern of thinking. This process of "creative destruction" is today a well-accepted theory of societal change, first introduced by German sociologist Werner Sombart and elaborated and popularized by Austrian economist Joseph

Schumpeter. We cannot, to a paraphrase Einstein, solve today's problems with yesterday's thinking.

Business is naturally creative and innovative. What is different about the Age of Responsibility is that business creativity needs to be directed to solving the world's social and environmental problems. Apple, for example, is highly creative, but their iPhone does little to tackle our most pressing societal needs. By contrast, Vodafone's M-PESA innovation by Safaricom in Kenya, which allows money to be transferred by text, empowered a nation in which 80% of the population had no bank account and where more money flows into the country through international remittances than foreign aid. Or consider Freeplay's innovation, using battery-free wind-up technology for torches, radios and laptops in Africa, thereby giving millions of people access to products and services in areas that are off the electricity grid.

All of these are part of the exciting trend towards social enterprise or social business that is sweeping the globe, supported by the likes of American Swiss entrepreneur Stephen Schmidheiny, Ashoka's Bill Drayton, eBay's Jeff Skoll, the World Economic Forum's Klaus Schwabb, Grameen Bank's Muhammad Yunus and Volans Venture's John Elkington. It is not a panacea, but for some products and services, directing the creativity of business towards the most pressing needs of society is the most rapid, scalable way to usher in the Age of Responsibility.

Practical steps to increase creativity include:

- Building social and environmental criteria into the core R&D function, as Nike has done with its Considered Design, and open sourcing patents, as Tesla Motors has done.

- Having forums, suggestion boxes and competitions where employees and other stakeholders can have their innovative ideas recognized and rewarded.

- Actively supporting, investing in and partnering with social enterprises, social entrepreneurs and "intrapreneurs" (entrepreneurs within the organization).

- Having diverse stakeholder representation on advisory boards and non-executive directors that can challenge the status quo.

- Fostering leaders that do not punish mistakes, but rather encourage a culture of experimentation and learning.

The principle of scalability in CSR 2.0

The CSR literature is liberally sprinkled with charming case studies of truly responsible and sustainable projects and a few pioneering companies. The problem is that so few of them ever go to scale. It is almost as if, once the sound bites and PR plaudits have been achieved, no further action is required. They become shining pilot projects and best practice examples, tarnished only by the fact that they are endlessly repeated on the CSR conference circuits of the world, without any vision for how they might transform the core business of their progenitors.

The sustainability problems we face, be they climate change or poverty, are at such a massive scale, and are so urgent, that any CSR solutions that cannot match that scale and urgency are red herrings at best and evil diversions at worst. How long have we been tinkering away with ethical consumerism (organic, fair trade and the like), with hardly any impact on the world's major corporations or supply chains? And yet, when Walmart's former CEO, Lee Scott, had his post-Katrina Damascus experience and decided that all fish would be MSC-certified, then we started seeing CSR 2.0-type scalability.

Scalability is not limited to the retail sector. In financial services, there have always been charitable loans for the world's poor and destitute. But when Muhammad Yunus, in the aftermath of a devastating famine in Bangladesh, set up the Grameen Bank and it went from one $74 loan in 1974 to a $2.5 billion enterprise, spawning more than 3,000 similar microcredit institutions in 50 countries reaching over 133 million clients, that is a lesson in scalability. Or contrast Toyota's laudable but premium-priced hybrid Prius for the rich and eco-conscious with a cheap and eco-friendly car for the masses, such as the Nissan Leaf. The one is an incremental solution with long-term potential; the other is scalable solution with immediate impact.

Practical steps to increase scalability include:

- Embracing sustainable or ethical choice, editing product line by product line, as Sainsbury's has done, beginning with fair-trade bananas.

- Having a programme of best-practice transfer within the organization, where small, successful sustainability solutions can be replicated more widely.

- Collaborating within sectors to raise the standards within an industry, such as the detoxification programme among textiles companies.

- Participating in cross-sector knowledge sharing forums in order to spread successful practices to other industries, such as the Water Footprint Network and WBCSD's Greenhouse Gas Protocol.

- Working with supply chains, as Walmart is doing with its Sustainability Index, and with customers, as Unilever is doing with its Sustainable Living Plan, and with bottom of the pyramid markets, as Ashoka is doing with its Hybrid Value Chain model—to encourage behaviour change en masse.

The principle of responsiveness in CSR 2.0

Business has a long track record of responsiveness to community needs—witness generations of philanthropy and heart-warming generosity following disasters such as 9/11 or the Sichuan Earthquake. But this is responsiveness on business's own terms, responsiveness when giving is easy and cheque-writing does nothing to upset their commercial applecart. The severity of the global problems we face demands that companies go much further. CSR 2.0 requires uncomfortable, transformative responsiveness, which questions whether the industry or the business model itself is part of the solution or part of the problem.

When it became clear that climate change posed a serious challenge to the sustainability of the fossil fuel industry, all the major oil companies formed the Global Climate Coalition, a lobby group explicitly designed to discredit and deny the science of climate change and undermine the main international policy response, the Kyoto Protocol. In typical CSR 1.0 style, these same companies were simultaneously making hollow claims about their CSR credentials. By contrast, the Prince of Wales's Corporate Leaders Group on Climate Change has, since 2005, been lobbying for bolder UK, EU and international legislation on climate change, accepting that carbon emission reductions of 50–85% will be needed by 2050.

CSR 2.0 responsiveness also means greater transparency, not only through reporting mechanisms such as the Global Reporting Initiative and Carbon Disclosure Project, but also by sharing critical intellectual resources. The Eco-Patent Commons, set up by WBCSD to make technology patents available, without royalty, to help reduce waste, pollution, global warming and energy demands, is one such step in the right direction. Another is the donor exchange platforms such as Give Aid Direct, allowing individual and corporate donors to connect directly with beneficiaries via the web, thereby tapping "the long tail of CSR".

Practical steps to increase responsiveness include:

- Adopting "impact investing" principles that assess the effectiveness of philanthropic and community development expenditures.

- Institutionalizing a variety of stakeholder panels to give honest feedback regarding the organization's sustainability performance.

- Engaging in positive, constructive policy lobbying on strategic social and environmental issues, as Seventh Generation has done on product labelling for household cleaning products.

- Embracing Web 2.0 approaches such as social media and crowd-sourcing to improve transparency, as sites such as Convetit have facilitated.

- Actively working to advance integrated reporting and full-cost accounting, as Puma has done with its Environmental Profit and Loss account, and ContextReporting.org is doing with its benchmarking platform.

The principle of glocality in CSR 2.0

The term glocalization comes from the Japanese word *dochakuka*, which simply means global localization. Originally referring to a way of adapting farming techniques to local conditions, *dochakuka* evolved into a marketing strategy when Japanese businessmen adopted it in the 1980s. It was subsequently introduced and popularized in the West in the 1990s by Manfred Lange, Roland Robertson, Keith Hampton, Barry Wellman and Zygmunt Bauman.

In a CSR context, the idea of "think global, act local" recognizes that most CSR issues manifest as dilemmas, rather than easy choices. In a complex, interconnected CSR 2.0 world, companies (and their critics) will have to become far more sophisticated in understanding local contexts and finding the appropriate local solutions they demand, without forsaking universal principles.

For example, a few years ago, BHP Billiton was vexed by their relatively poor performance on a CSR Index, run by UK charity Business in the

Community. Further analysis showed that the company had been marked down for their high energy use and relative energy inefficiency. Fair enough. Or was it? Most of BHP Billiton's operations were, at that time, based in southern Africa, home to some of the world's cheapest electricity. No wonder this was not a high priority. What was a priority, however, was controlling malaria in the community, where they had made a huge positive impact. But the CSR Index didn't have any rating questions on malaria, so this was ignored. Instead, it demonstrated a typical, West-driven, one-size-fits-all CSR 1.0 approach.

By contrast, in a sugar farming co-operative in Guatemala, they have their own CSR pyramid—economic responsibility is still the platform, but rather than legal, ethical and philanthropic dimensions, their pyramid includes responsibility to the family (of employees), the community and policy engagement. Hence, CSR 2.0 replaces "either/or" with "both/and" thinking. Both SA 8000 and the Chinese national labour standard have their role to play. Both premium branded and cheap generic drugs have a place in the solution to global health issues. CSR 2.0 is a search for the Chinese concept of a harmonious society, which implies a dynamic yet productive tension of opposites—a Tai Chi of CSR, balancing *yin* and *yang*.

Practical steps to increase glocality include:

- Publicly committing to follow with global best practice principles and standards, such as the UN Global Compact or ISO 26000.

- Ensuring that community groups and local civil society organizations are consulted on all major developments that affect them, for example using environmental and social impact assessments.

- Entering into Global MOU agreements with communities to agree performance targets, as Chevron and Shell do in Nigeria.

- Having an active employee secondment and volunteer programme, which allows cross-cultural and cross-national knowledge transfer with the organization and greater sensitivity to local challenges.

- Developing clear policy guidelines and procedures on how values translate into practice, as Anglo American does for example on issues surrounding bribery and corruption.

The principle of circularity in CSR 2.0

The reason CSR 1.0 has failed is not through lack of good intent, nor even through lack of effort. The old CSR has failed because our global economic system is based on a fundamentally flawed design. For all the miraculous energy unleashed by Adam Smith's (1982) "invisible hand" of the free market, our modern capitalist system is faulty at its very core. Simply put, it is conceived as an abstract system without limits. As far back as the 1960s, pioneering economist, Kenneth Boulding, called this a "cowboy economy", where endless frontiers imply no limits on resource consumption or waste disposal. By contrast, he argued, we need to design a "spaceship economy", where there is no "away"; everything is engineered to constantly recycle.

In the 1990s, in *The Ecology of Commerce*, Paul Hawken (1993) translated these ideas into three basic rules for sustainability: waste equals food; nature runs off current solar income; and nature depends on diversity. He also proposed replacing our product-sales economy with a service-lease model, famously using the example of Interface "Evergreen" carpets that are leased and constantly replaced and recycled. Michael Braungart and William McDonough (2008) have extended this thinking in their *Cradle to Cradle* industrial model. Cradle to cradle is not only about closing the loop on production, but about designing for "good", rather than the CSR 1.0 modus operandi of "less bad".

Hence, CSR 2.0 circularity would, according to circular economy aspirations, create buildings that, like trees, produce more energy than they consume and purify their own waste-water; or factories that produce drinking water as effluent; or products that decompose and become food and nutrients; or materials that can feed into industrial cycles as high-quality raw materials for new products. Circularity needn't only apply to the environment. Business should be constantly feeding and replenishing its social and human capital, not only through education and training, but also by nourishing community and employee wellbeing. CSR 2.0 raises the importance of meaning in work and life to equal status alongside ecological integrity and financial viability.

Practical steps to increase circularity include:

- Conducting life-cycle impact assessments on all significant products and services to understand their Cradle to Cradle impacts.

- Embracing product footprinting and labelling techniques, such as Tesco has done with carbon labelling and Patagonia has done with its Footprint Chronicles.

- Providing, or partnering to provide, product take-back, recycling and upcycling schemes, such as Fonebak does with mobile phones and Fuji Xerox does with printers.

- Publicly committing to BHAGS (big hairy audacious goals)—what Interface calls Mission Zero, the sportswear industry calls the Race to Zero and John Elkington (2012) calls the *Zeronauts* revolution.

- Working to create industrial ecology parks, where waste output from process is designed to be resource inputs into other processes, as is the case with the town Kalundborg in Denmark.

Making the shift to transformative CSR

Revolutions involve transition. What markers can we expect to see on the transformational road? Table 4 summarizes the shifts in the defining features between CSR 1.0 and CSR 2.0.

Paternalistic relationships, based on philanthropy, between companies and the community, give way to more equal partnerships. Defensive, minimalist responses to social and environmental issues are replaced with proactive strategies and investment in growing responsibility markets, such as clean technology. As reputation-conscious public relations approaches to CSR lose credibility, companies are judged on actual social, environmental

CSR 1.0	CSR 2.0
Philanthropic	Collaborative
Risk-based	Reward-based
Image-driven	Performance-driven
Specialized	Integrated
Standardized	Diversified
Marginal	Scalable
Western	Global

TABLE 4   Shifting CSR features

CSR 1.0	CSR 2.0
CSR premium	Base of the pyramid
Charity projects	Social enterprise
CSR indexes	CSR ratings
CSR departments	CSR incentives
Product liability	Choice editing
Ethical consumerism	Service agreements
CSR reporting cycles	CSR data streams
Stakeholder groups	Social networks
Process standards	Performance standards

TABLE 5   Shifting CSR practices

and ethical performance (are things getting better on the ground in absolute, cumulative terms?).

How might these shifting features manifest as CSR practices? Table 5 summarizes key changes in the way in which CSR will be visibly operationalized.

Hence, CSR will no longer be limited to luxury products and services (as with current green and fair-trade options). Instead, it will grow to encompass affordable solutions for those who most need quality of life improvements. For example, the way Nestlé has fortified their Popularly Positioned Products (PPPs) such as the Maggie range, and Danone has fortified their yogurts in partnership with the Grameen Group.

Investment in social enterprises that are self-sustaining will be favoured over cheque-book charity. For example, there are 235 organizations from 58 countries that now support the World Toilet Organization. One of them, Index Award (the world's biggest design award body) helped to design a SaniShop franchise to brand and design flat-pack sanitation products for scaling up distribution in the developing world (Sim, 2011).

CSR indexes (that currently rank a limited set of large corporations) will make way for CSR rating systems that translate social, environmental, ethical and economic performance into corporate scores (similar to credit ratings) which can be employed by analysts and others in their decision-making. Hence the Global 100 "Most Sustainable Corporations in the World" ranking is much less useful for investors than MSCI's ESG ratings, based on analysts reviewing more than 500 data points and score more than 100 indicators, to score companies on a nine-point scale from AAA to C.

Reliance on CSR departments will diminish, as responsibility and sustainability performance is incorporated into organizational appraisal and market incentive systems. This is one of ten steps to embed sustainability within an organization of The Prince's Accounting for Sustainability Project (A4S). For example, the Argentine confectionery company, Arcor, includes sustainability in the performance appraisals of all of their top management, and Xcel Energy links bonuses to carbon reduction and safety performance.

CSR 2.0 companies will "choice edit" (i.e. cease to offer "less ethical" products), thus allowing guilt-free shopping. For example, British retailer Iceland adopted a policy of GMO-free for all its food products, while The Body Shop has a "no animal testing" policy for all of its cosmetics products. Other examples include Unilever, McDonald's and Nestlé, as well as the country of Belgium, which have all committed to sourcing only Roundtable on Sustainable Palm Oil (RSPO) certified palm oil by 2015.

Post-use liability for products will become obsolete, as the service-lease and take-back economy becomes mainstream. Interface was one of the pioneers when it offered its Evergreen Lease carpets, so that all maintenance and recycling was the company's responsibility. A more recent example is Zipcar, the world's largest car sharing and car club service, which provides an alternative to traditional car rental and car ownership. In the electronics industry, Cisco and others have Takeback and Recycle schemes to close the loop on production.

Web 2.0 connected social networks that facilitate crowdsourcing will replace periodic meetings of cumbersome stakeholder panels. For example, General Electric (GE) used Convetit's sustainability expert crowdsourcing platform to get critical feedback on its Corporate Citizenship report before it was finalized and published. GlaxoSmithKline (GSK) has used the open source wiki principle to create its Patent Pool for tropic diseases. Wikirate allows stakeholders to publicly and dynamically update their views on organizations' sustainability performance.

CSR 1.0 management systems standards such as ISO 14001 will be replaced with (or complemented by) new performance standards, such as those emerging in climate change that set absolute limits and thresholds. The problem with process standards is that organizations set their own voluntary (and often unambitious) targets, irrespective of the scale and urgency of the challenge. By contrast, standards such as SA 8000, "carbon neutral", "water neutral" or "zero waste" set quantified minimum performance requirements.

Decoding the new DNA of business

All of these visions of the future imply such a radical shift from the current model of CSR that they beg the question: do we need a new model of CSR? Academic Archie Carroll's (1991) enduring CSR Pyramid, with its Western cultural assumptions, static design and wholesale omission of environmental issues is no longer fit for purpose. Even the emphasis on "social" in corporate social responsibility implies a rather limited view of the agenda. So what might a new model look like?

The CSR 2.0 model proposes that we keep the acronym, but rebalance the scales. CSR comes to stand for "Corporate Sustainability and Responsibility". This change acknowledges that sustainability (with roots in the environmental movement) and responsibility (with roots in the social activist movement) are the two main games in town. A cursory look at companies' nonfinancial reports will rapidly confirm this—they are mostly either corporate sustainability or corporate responsibility reports.

CSR 2.0 also proposes a new interpretation of the terms. Like two intertwined strands of DNA, sustainability and responsibility can be thought of as different, yet complementary elements of CSR. Hence, sustainability should be seen as a destination—the challenges, vision, strategy and goals that we are aiming for, while responsibility is about the journey—solutions, responses, management and actions that show how we get there.

The DNA of CSR 2.0 represents a new holistic model of CSR. The essence of the CSR 2.0 DNA model are the four DNA Responsibility Bases, which are like the four nitrogenous bases of biological DNA (adenine, cytosine, guanine, and thymine), sometimes abbreviated to the four letters GCTA (which was the inspiration for the 1997 science fiction film *GATTACA*). In the case of CSR 2.0, the DNA Responsibility Bases are Value creation, Good governance, Societal contribution and Environmental integrity.

Hence, if we look at **value creation**, it is clear we are talking about more than financial profitability. The goal is economic development, which means not only contributing to the enrichment of shareholders and executives, but improving the economic context in which a company operates, including investing in infrastructure, creating jobs, providing skills development and so on. There can be any number of KPIs, but I want to highlight two that I believe are essential: beneficial products and inclusive business. Does the company's products and services really improve our quality of life, or do they cause harm or add to the low-quality junk of what Charles Handy calls the "*chindogu* society". And how are the economic benefits shared?

Does wealth trickle up or down; are employees, SMEs in the supply chain and poor communities genuinely empowered?

Good governance is another area that is not new, but in my view has failed to be properly recognized or integrated in CSR circles. The goal of institutional effectiveness is as important as more lofty social and environmental ideals. After all, if the institution fails, or is not transparent and fair, this undermines everything else that CSR is trying to accomplish. Trends in reporting, but also other forms of transparency such as social media and brand- or product-linked public databases of CSR performance, will be increasingly important indicators of success, alongside embedding ethical conduct in the culture of companies. Tools such as GoodGuide, KPMG's Integrity Thermometer and Covalence's EthicalQuote ranking will become more prevalent.

Societal contribution is an area that CSR is traditionally more used to addressing, with its goal of stakeholder orientation. This gives philanthropy its rightful place in CSR—as one tile in a larger mosaic—while also providing a spotlight for the importance of fair labour practices. It is simply unacceptable that there are more people in slavery today than there were before it was officially abolished in the 1800s, just as regular exposures continue to reveal the despicable use of child labour by high-brand companies. This area of stakeholder engagement, community participation and supply chain integrity remains one of the most vexing and critical elements of CSR.

Finally, **environmental integrity** sets the bar way higher than minimizing damage and rather aims at maintaining and improving ecosystem sustainability. The KPIs give some sense of the ambition required here—100% renewable energy and zero waste. We cannot continue the same practices that have, according to WWF's Living Planet Index, caused us to lose more than half of the populations of vertebrates on the planet since they began monitoring in 1970. Nor can we continue to gamble with prospect of dangerous—and perhaps catastrophic and irreversible—climate change.

CSR 2.0 is, at its core, clarification and reorientation of the purpose of business. It is a misnomer to believe that the purpose of business is to be profitable, or to serve shareholders. These are simply means to an end. Ultimately, the purpose of business is to serve society, through the provision of safe, high-quality products and services that enhance our wellbeing, without the erosion of our ecological and community life-support systems. The essence of CSR 2.0 is positive contribution to society—not as a marginal afterthought, but as a way of business.

First steps towards CSR 2.0

To take the first steps, we must understand how to overcome resistance to change. Richard Beckhard and David Gleicher's Formula for Change states that: D x V x F > R, where D = Dissatisfaction with how things are now; V = Vision of what is possible; F = First concrete steps that can be taken towards the vision; and R = Resistance to change (Beckhard and Harris, 1987). In terms of CSR and sustainability, the weakest variable is D, i.e. dissatisfaction with the status quo. This requires connecting people to the impacts of their actions, using tools such as footprinting (for ecological, carbon and water), life-cycle assessment and supply chain auditing.

The evolution from CSR 1.0 to CSR 2.0 will be a long and bloody battle. In my own experience, as a South African, it took over 40 years of sustained and organized protest to change the entrenched power of the apartheid government, especially given the powerful vested interests of big companies. The Occupy movement is one important indicator that the element (D) is changing in a way that is favourable for CSR 2.0 and ought to be encouraged and sustained.

In terms of first steps, I recommend five actions to organizations that genuinely want to move from CSR 1.0 to CSR 2.0:

1. **Reassess**: this is about taking stock of the social, environmental and ethical impacts of company, i.e. creating a sustainability and responsibility performance baseline. Sustainability guidelines by the Global Reporting Initiative (GRI), Carbon Disclosure Project (CDP) and the International Integrated Reporting Council (IIRC) are a good place to start, although ultimately this should embrace life-cycle impact assessment (which resulted in BASF switching to recyclable Nylon 6), and full-cost accounting (long used at companies such as Ontario Hydro and Baxter International).

2. **Realign**: this is about rethinking what cross-sector partnerships will shift perceptions and practices. In line with the 8th Millennium Development Goal (MDG), organizations need to find partners in business, government and civil society that will complement internal capabilities, while challenging the status quo. Examples include Rio Tinto partnering with the World Conservation Union (IUCN) to address biodiversity impacts and Unilever partnering with UNICEF, Oxfam, PSI, Save the Children and the

World Food Programme to help improve the lives of more than a billion people worldwide.

3. **Redefine:** this is about bold leadership, in particular setting a vision and strategic goals for the organization, which will inspire and challenge all stakeholders. Examples include former CEO of Walmart, Lee Scott, setting three sustainability goals for the company, including 100% renewable energy, zero waste and making all products sustainable. Interface's Mission Zero set by Ray Anderson, Unilever's Sustainable Living Plan set by Paul Polman and STMicroelectronics' Carbon Neutral strategy set by Pasquale Pistorio are other cases in point.

4. **Redesign:** this is about innovation, especially redesigning products and services to have minimal negative impact. Some companies are taking inspiration from Janine Benyus's concept of biomimicry (learning from nature's designs), such as Interface's "gekko foot" non-glue adhesive tiles, while others are challenged by C.K. Prahalad and Stuart Hart's concept of bottom of the pyramid (serving the poor), such as BP's Oorja low-smoke stove, or Vodafone's M-PESA financial texting service.

5. **Restructure:** this is about transformation of the context in which organizations operate, i.e. changing the rules of the game, especially the policy environment. For example, supporting bold climate change policies to ensure a carbon price and efficient carbon trading, as the CEOs of the EU Corporate Leaders Group on Climate Change have done. Or working on ingredient labels and salt, fat and sugar level disclosures for food manufacturers and retailers, or product take-back schemes in the electronics industry.

At the heart of the transformational nature of CSR 2.0 is the need to embrace long-term capitalism. This means testing all economic activity against five principles of Responsible Capitalism:

1. **Investment:** ensuring that money is channelled towards productive investments and not into speculative trading in the casino economy, as the Co-operative Bank has demonstrated successfully.

2. **Long termism:** understanding that real wealth is created by taking a long-term perspective, including the needs of future generations,

as Generation Investment and Warren Buffet's Berkshire Hathaway practice.

3. **Transparency**: embracing transparency in revenues, in line with the Global Reporting Initiative, Carbon Disclosure Project and Extractive Industries Transparency Initiative (EITI).

4. **Full-cost accounting**: internalizing social and environmental costs (externalities), either through taxes (e.g. on carbon and pollution) and social and environmental profit and loss accounts (e.g. Puma).

5. **Inclusion**: enacting Michael Porter's and Mark Kramer's concept of creating shared value, and serving the bottom of the pyramid (BOP) markets, as demonstrated by the BOP 2.0 Protocol.

We live in exciting times—a true period of bifurcation. We live on the cusp of the post-industrial revolution, and for the first time, we can finally glimpse what a new model of sustainable business and purpose-inspired capitalism could look like. As with so many things in life, the quest for a sustainable future is like a wheelbarrow. The only way we will make progress is if we pick it up and push forward. And the only way we will motivate people to join us in this effort is if they believe in what we are building. And what are we building? We are building nothing less than a new form of capitalism—one that serves society and sustains the planet.

Towards responsible competitiveness?

A few years ago, I was invited to make a presentation on CSR in Brussels to the EU High Level Group (HLG) on CSR, comprising 27 Member State representatives. The topic of my presentation was "CSR and the global financial crisis", and it gave me a fantastic opportunity to talk with some of the people helping to shape the EU agenda. There were a number of trends that I found interesting.

The first was that, whereas formerly CSR was discussed purely as a voluntary activity by business (this was especially clear in the EU's policy statement on CSR in 2006), there was now increasing discussion and even demand for what Susan Bird, CSR co-ordinator in the Directorate-General for Employment of the European Commission and part of the EU HLG on CSR, called "a more active role", which may involve "conditions" being introduced in the future, although this was all still up for debate.

A second insight was how the competitiveness agenda has changed. The first ten-year economic strategy of the European Union—the Lisbon Agenda, which ended in 2010—was all about competitiveness and paid very little attention to CSR issues. However, the 2008 European Competitiveness Report dedicated an entire chapter to CSR and countries such as Denmark were claiming that responsible, green growth was central to its international reputation and hence its competitiveness. This changing emphasis is also reflected in the new Lisbon Strategy for 2020, which has as its central goal "smart, sustainable and inclusive growth".

One of the people who has done the most work on responsible competitiveness is Simon Zadek. In 2010, I had the pleasure of visiting him in the lakeside city of Geneva, when he was still CEO of AccountAbility. The purpose of my visit was to interview Zadek about his book, *The Civil Corporation* (Zadek, 2001). This formed part of a research project I was conducting for the University of Cambridge, which resulted in the publication of *The Top 50 Sustainability Books* (Visser and CPSL, 2009).

Reflecting back on the book, and on what has changed since, Zadek pointed to the geopolitical shift towards Asia and Russia, the increasing influence of investment markets, the re-emergence of a strong state role and greater emphasis on partnerships and collaboration. I asked him what had prompted his more recent focus on responsible competitiveness. Zadek explained that it emerged largely as a response to the views of David Henderson, expressed in his book, *Misguided Virtue: False Notions of Corporate Social Responsibility* (Henderson, 2001).

Henderson (2001) argued that corporate responsibility increased poverty, because it reduced market flexibility and added costs, whereas markets were the route to prosperity. "It was a rather caricatured view of everything," claimed Zadek. "But the underlying point made came through to me, which was: what are the macroeconomic effects? We've all been concentrating on the micro side." Zadek began to realize that "micro-level innovation would be halted if the national policy implications of advancing corporate responsibility at the micro-level would undermine national or regional competitiveness. So to understand the political economy of corporate responsibility or sustainability or citizenship required an understanding where national competitive strategies and the political dimensions of that 'hit the road' on this agenda."

To illustrate what he meant, Zadek noted that "the debate about a post-Kyoto deal is a debate about competitiveness. What's going to prevent it moving on is a zero sum view without a pay-off matrix; that is about a loss of competitiveness at both the top of the economic pyramid and mid and low levels in the pyramid."

I pushed him to elaborate. "Climate change is the perfect storm," he said. "It is credible systemic risk accompanied by demonstrable failure of our two primary large-scale instruments of change, namely public policy and capital market allocation. Because public policy is not reshaping markets to be forward looking at anything like the pace that's needed, and capital markets are not recognizing the value-added opportunities, or factoring them into their asset valuation methodologies. And so at that point the importance of collaboration, new models of partnerships, new ways of constructing market rules, becomes the game."

I think Singapore can give further insights on responsible competitiveness, especially around the issues of water and human resources. It was only after a political crisis with Malaysia that Singapore instituted the range of measures, including leading-edge filtration and desalination technologies that now make it not only virtually water self-sufficient, but also a leading exporter of water technologies. I did hear talk of Singapore becoming a green IT or cleantech hub for Asia, but I think the government's softly-softly approach will leave it far in the wake of countries such as South Korea, Japan and China.

Even so, there is a lesson to be learned from Singapore. As a geographically small city-state, with a relatively high population density, the government quickly faced up to the fact that there is no "away". It had to deal with its own externalities, rather than export them. Innovation was born of necessity. Poverty and pollution could not be tucked away in remote rural regions or ignored as the inevitable lot of a fringe slum society. Either the whole city prospered, or it didn't. There was nowhere to hide poor governance.

As the Asian tigers jockeyed for position in the region and the world in the 1980s and 1990s, Singapore made strategic investments in two areas—its people (creating a highly skilled labour force) and its infrastructure (making it one of the most friendly trade and investment hubs in the world). Singapore knew that if it didn't get these two things right, it would have no competitive advantage. Most crucially, it would lose its upwardly mobile workforce to Japan, South Korea or the West, and global economic activity would divert to other parts of Asia.

We can all learn from this "spaceship earth" (city-state) thinking of Singapore. But, for me, the jury is still out on responsible competitiveness. Unless the governments and companies around the world can shake off the "competitiveness at all costs" mentality, they will always be a responsible business laggard, moving with the late majority; certainly not the worst, but far from the best.

7
Unlocking change through integrated value

Creating shared value: revolution or clever con?

Many argue that CSR and sustainability are not the way to unlock change. I have been one of the critics, while still believing that reform is possible. More recently, however, the most vocal critic has been Harvard professor Michael Porter. "The capitalist system is under siege," he claimed in an article in *Harvard Business Review* in 2011, co-authored with management consultant Mark Kramer.

> In recent years business increasingly has been viewed as a major cause of social, environmental, and economic problems. Companies are widely perceived to be prospering at the expense of the broader community. Even worse, the more business has begun to embrace corporate responsibility, the more it has been blamed for society's failures. (Porter and Kramer, 2011)

The problem, according to Porter and Kramer, is that companies remain trapped in an outdated approach to value creation. They continue to view value creation narrowly, optimizing short-term financial performance in a bubble while missing the most important customer needs and ignoring the broader influences that determine their longer-term success.

As far as solutions go, Porter and Kramer (2011) see CSR as something of a red herring, despite the authors having written a previous paper in *Harvard Business Review* in 2006 extolling CSR as a route to competitiveness. Now they see CSR as a "mind-set in which societal issues are at the periphery, not the core" and "a reaction to external pressure—[which has] emerged largely to improve firms' reputations".

By contrast, they argue that the principle of shared value involves creating economic value in a way that also creates value for society by addressing its needs and challenges:

> Businesses must reconnect company success with social progress. Shared value is not social responsibility, philanthropy, or even sustainability, but a new way to achieve economic success. It is not on the margin of what companies do but at the center.

This redefinition of corporate purpose from profit maximization to shared value creation—which the authors claim is starting to be embraced by the likes of GE, Google, IBM, Intel, Johnson & Johnson, Nestlé, Unilever and Walmart—requires "a far deeper appreciation of societal needs, a greater understanding of the true bases of company productivity, and the ability to collaborate across profit/nonprofit boundaries".

And how can companies create shared value? There are three distinct ways, according to the authors: by reconceiving products and markets, redefining productivity in the value chain, and building supportive industry clusters at the company's locations. "Each of these is part of the virtuous circle of shared value; improving value in one area gives rise to opportunities in the others."

Porter and Kramer are keen to emphasize that shared value is not about sharing the value already created by firms—a redistribution approach. Instead, it is about expanding the total pool of economic and social value. They illustrate this with the example of cocoa farmers in the Côte d'Ivoire, where fair trade can increase farmers' incomes by 10% to 20%, while shared value investments can raise their incomes by more than 300%.

If we succeed, Porter and Kramer (2011) believe this shared value approach will drive the next wave of innovation and productivity growth, reshape capitalism and its relationship to society, and legitimize business again.

However, the question is whether CSR and CSV (creating shared value) are really different? In fact, is CSV even a new concept, or just old wine in new wineskins? Porter and Kramer (2011) also argue that CSV is more preferable than fair trade. Is that true? I want to tackle some of these questions, as well as reflect on the true value of CSV and the future of CSR.

The first thing to place on record is that CSV reflects an evolution in Porter and Kramer's (2011) own thinking. After a career spent focusing on economic competitiveness devoid of any consideration of social impacts, Porter teamed up with Kramer in 2002 to write about "the competitive advantage of corporate philanthropy", which they then reframed in 2006 as "strategic CSR". Hence, CSV is their third foray into the field of social responsibility—which rather ironically and explicitly disparages the previous two.

The second point is that CSV is nothing new. At the very least, we can say that it strongly echoes the work of C.K. Prahalad and Stuart Hart on serving markets at the "bottom of the pyramid" (BOP) (Prahalad and Hart, 2002), as well as the idea of supporting "inclusive business"—something into which the International Finance Corporation (IFC) has channelled $7 billion in over 80 countries since 2005. It is somewhat disingenuous and poor academic form that these foundational concepts were not even acknowledged by Porter and Kramer.

The third aspect of CSV that I take issue with is the way in which the duo characterize corporate social responsibility. I agree that some companies are still practising an immature form of CSR—which I have called CSR 1.0—that is defensive and risk-based, philanthropic-oriented or PR-driven. However, numerous companies have moved on to a fourth stage—strategic CSR, as exemplified by the ISO 26000 standard—and some have even gone beyond that, to what I call transformative CSR, or CSR 2.0.

Not content to discredit social responsibility alone, Porter and Kramer (2011) also launch an attack on the fair-trade movement, which they say "is mostly about redistribution rather than expanding the overall amount of value created". By contrast, CSV:

> focuses on improving growing techniques and strengthening the local cluster of supporting suppliers and other institutions in order to increase farmers' efficiency, yields, product quality, and sustainability. This leads to a bigger pie of revenue and profits that benefits both farmers and the companies that buy from them.

The fact that these aspects are integral to the work that the Fairtrade Foundation seems to have been conveniently overlooked.

Having said all that, if my short critical tirade has given the impression that I am against CSV, allow me to set the record straight: I am a CSV fan, and here are the reasons why: I believe it has injected a new energy into the CSR movement. It has cleverly changed the language of social responsibility into the language of value creation, which business leaders can better understand and it has challenged the narrow definition of corporate purpose to go beyond profit maximization. What is more, it has rightly advocated a better alignment between a company's core strategy and the social problems that it can have an impact on.

At the end of the day, I am less concerned about the labels we use—be it CSR, BOP, corporate citizenship, sustainability or CSV—and more interested in whether the concept and practice are holistic and transformative. This means business has to embrace what I described in the previous chapter as the four DNA elements of responsibility: value creation, good governance, societal contribution and environmental integrity. It also means applying creativity, scalability, responsiveness, glocality and circularity to the business solutions to society's needs. And yes, it means calling for a transformation of capitalism—which I am pleased to see Porter and Kramer (2011) agree with.

Creating integrated value: beyond CSR and CSV

My criticism of CSV is that it does not go far enough. It is actually a rather narrow concept, focusing on the win–win areas of when social and economic value overlap. I believe the next step—the evolution of CSR and CSV, if you like—is Creating Integrated Value, or CIV, which I have developed with global quality expert and author of *Integrated Management Systems*, Chad Kymal (Kymal *et al.*, 2015).

Integrated Value is a concept and practice that has emerged from a long tradition of thinking on the role of business in society. It has its roots in what many today call corporate (social) responsibility or CSR, corporate citizenship, business ethics and corporate sustainability. These ideas also have a long history, but can be seen to have evolved primarily along two strands—let's call them streams of consciousness: the responsibility stream and the sustainability stream.

The responsibility stream had its origins in the mid- to late 1800s, with industrialists such as John D. Rockefeller and Dale Carnegie setting a precedent for community philanthropy, while others such as John Cadbury and John H. Patterson seeded the employee welfare movement. Fast forward a hundred years or so, and we see the first social responsibility codes start to emerge, such as the Sullivan Principles in 1977, and the subsequent steady march of standardization, giving us SA 8000 (1997), ISO 26000 (2010) and many others.

The sustainability stream also started early, with air pollution regulation in the UK and land conservation in the USA in the 1870s. Fast forward by a century and we get the first Earth Day, Greenpeace and the UN Stockholm

Conference on Environment and Development. By the 1980s and 1990s, we have the Brundtland definition of "sustainable development" (1987), the Valdez Principles (1989, later called the CERES Principles) and the Rio Earth Summit (1992), tracking through to standards such as ISO 14001 (1996).

As these two movements of responsibility and sustainability gathered momentum, they naturally began to see their interconnectedness. Labour rights connected with human rights, quality connected with health and safety, community connected with supply chain, environment connected with productivity, and so on. The coining of the "triple bottom line" of economic, social and environmental performance by John Elkington in 1994, and the introduction of the ten principles of the UN Global Compact in 1999 reflected this trend.

We also saw integration start to happen at a more practical level. The ISO 9001 quality standard became the design template for ISO 14001 on environmental management and OHSAS 18001 on occupational health and safety. The Global Reporting Initiative and the Dow Jones Sustainability Index adopted the triple bottom line lens. Fair-trade certification incorporated economic, social and environmental concerns, and even social responsibility evolved into a more holistic concept, now encapsulated in the seven core subjects of ISO 26000.

At every stage in this process, there have been those who have challenged our understanding of the scope and ambition of corporate responsibility and sustainability. Ed Freeman introduced us to stakeholder theory in 1984, John Elkington to the triple bottom line in 1994, Rosabeth Moss Kanter to social innovation in 1999, Jed Emerson to blended value in 2000, C.K. Prahalad and Stuart Hart to bottom of the pyramid (BOP) inclusive markets in 2004, and Michael Porter and Mark Kramer to creating shared value (CSV) in 2011.

Typically, these new conceptions build on what went before, but call for greater integration and an expansion of the potential of business to make positive impacts. For example, Hart's "sustainable value" framework (2011) incorporates pollution prevention, product stewardship, base of the pyramid (BOP) and cleantech. Emerson's "blended value", much like Elkington's "triple bottom line" looks for an overlap between profit and social and environmental targets, while Porter and Kramer's CSV focuses on synergies between economic and social goals.

The "how to" of integration

Integrated Value takes inspiration from all of the thought pioneers that have gone before and tries to take the next step. CIV is not so much a new idea—as the longstanding trend towards integration and the ubiquitous call for embedding of standards testifies—but rather an attempt to work out the "how to" of integration. When companies are faced with a proliferation of standards (Standards Map alone profiles over 150 sustainability standards) and the multiplication of stakeholder expectations, how can they sensibly respond?

I have analysed some of the most important global guidelines, codes and standards covering the social, ethical and environmental responsi-bilities of business—such as the UN Global Compact, OECD Guidelines for Multinational Enterprises, ISO 26000, GRI Sustainability Reporting Guidelines (G4), IIRC Integrated Reporting Guidelines, SA 8000, UN Business and Human Rights Framework and Dow Jones Sustainability Index. What we see are large areas of overlap in these guidelines, codes and standards across what I have called the $S_2QuE_3LCH_2$ issues, namely:

- S_2: Safety and Social issues

- Qu: Quality issues

- E_3: Environmental, Economic and Ethical issues

- L: Labour issues

- C: Carbon or Climate issues

- H_2: Health and Human rights issues

Our experience of working with business shows that most companies respond piecemeal to this diversity and complexity of $S_2QuE_3LCH_2$ issues (let's call them SQuELCH for short). A few large corporations use a manage-ment systems approach to embed the requirements of whatever codes and standards they have signed up to. Even, so they tend to do this in silos—one set of people and systems for quality, another for health and safety, another for environment, and still others for employees, supply chain management and community issues.

CIV, therefore, is about knocking down the silos and finding ways to inte-grate across the business. In short, CIV helps a company to integrate its response to stakeholder expectations (using materiality analysis) through its management systems (using best governance practices) and value chain linkages (using life-cycle thinking). This integration is applied across critical processes in the business, such as governance and strategic planning, product/service development and delivery, and supply and customer chain management.

And what about value? Most crucially, CIV builds in an innovation step, so that redesigning products and processes to deliver solutions to the biggest social and environmental challenges we face can create new value. CIV also brings multiple business benefits, from reducing risks, costs, liabilities and audit fatigue to improving reputation, revenues, employee motivation, customer satisfaction and stakeholder relations.

Our experience with implementing and integrating existing standards such as ISO 9001 and ISO 14001 convinces us that, in order for CIV to work, leaders need to step up and create transformational goals. Without ambition "baked in" to CIV adoption, the resulting incremental improvements will be no match for the scale and urgency of the global social and environmental crises we face, such as climate change and growing inequality.

One of the most exciting transformational agendas right now is the Net Zero/Net Positive movement, which extends the "zero" mind-set of total quality management to other economic, social and environmental performance areas. For example, we see companies targeting zero waste, water and carbon; zero defects, accidents and missed customer commitments; and zero corruption, labour infringements and human rights violations. These kinds of zero stretch goal, adopted by what John Elkington calls *Zeronauts* (Elkington, 2012), defines what it means to be world class today.

Stepping up to integrated change

In practice, CIV implementation is a six-step process, which can be described as:

1. Listen Up! (stakeholder materiality)

2. Look Out! (integrated risk)

3. Dig Down! (critical processes)

4. Aim High! (innovation and value)

5. Line Up! (systems alignment)

6. Think Again! (audit and review)

Each step is briefly explained below. Of course, the process must also remain flexible enough to be adapted to each company context and to different industry sectors.

1. **Listen Up! (stakeholder materiality)**: the first step of the CIV process is Stakeholder Materiality Analysis, which systematically identifies and prioritizes all stakeholders—including customers, employees, shareholders, suppliers, regulators, communities and others—before mapping their needs and expectations and analysing their materiality to the business. This includes aligning with the strategic objectives of the organization and then driving through to result measurables, key processes and process measurables.

   The stakeholder materiality analysis is the first level of integration and should be conducted simultaneously for quality, cost, products, environment, health and safety and social responsibility. The analysis helps to shape a comprehensive set of goals and objectives, as well as the overall scorecard of the organization. When conducted holistically as a part of the organization's annual setting of goals, objectives and budgets, it seamlessly integrates into how the business operates. A similar approach was developed and fine-tuned by Omnex for Ford Motor Company in a process called the Quality Operating System.

2. **Look Out! (integrated risk)**: in parallel with the Stakeholder Materiality Analysis, the risks to the business are analysed through an Integrated Risk Assessment. This means the identification and quantification of quality, cost, product, environment, health and safety and social responsibility risks, in terms of their potential effect on the company's strategic, production, administrative and value chain processes. The risk measures developed need to be valid for all the different types of risk and different entities of the business, and mitigation measures identified.

   The first two steps of Stakeholder Analysis and Risk Assessment are requirements of the updated ISO 9001, ISO 14001 and new ISO 45001 (formerly OHSAS 18001) standards slated to come out in 2015. For example, in the new ISO 9001 that is planned for release in 2015, it is called "Understanding the Needs and Expectations of Interested Parties" and "Actions to Address Risks and Opportunities". The evolution of the ISO standards is indicative of a shift in global mind-set (since ISO represents over a hundred different countries) to prioritizing stakeholder engagement and risk management.

3. **Dig Deep! (critical processes)**: in Step 3, the Stakeholder Materiality Analysis and Integrated Risk Assessment are used to identify critical business processes, using the Process Map of the organization. It is likely that the most critical processes—in terms of their impact on SQuELCH issues—will include governance and strategic planning, product or service development, product or service delivery, supply chain management, and customer chain management. There may also be others, depending on the particular business or industry sector. This critical processes list should also include the most relevant subprocesses.

4. **Aim High! (innovation and value)**: Step 4 entails the Innovation and Value Identification element. Using the Net Zero/Net Positive strategic goals, or others such as Stuart Hart's sustainable value framework, each of the critical processes is analysed for opportunities to innovate. Opportunity analysis is followed by idea generation and screening and the creation of a Breakthrough List. This is the chance for problem-solving teams, Six Sigma teams, Lean teams, and Design for Six Sigma teams and others to use improvement tools to take the company towards its chosen transformational goals. The improvement projects will continue for a few months until they are implemented and put into daily practice.

5. **Line Up! (systems alignment)**: in Step 5, the requirements of the various SQuELCH standards most relevant for the organization, together with the transformational strategic goals, are integrated into the management system of the organization, including the business processes, work instructions and forms/checklists. Process owners working with cross-functional teams ensure that the organizational processes are capable of meeting the requirements defined by the various standards and strategic goals. This is followed by training to ensure that the new and updated processes are understood, implemented and being followed.

6. **Think Again! (audit and review)**: integration has one final step, Internal Audit and Management Review, which creates the feedback and continuous improvement loop that is essential for any successful management system. This means integrating the value creation process into the governance systems of organization,

including strategic planning and budgeting, management or business reviews, internal audits and corrective actions. This is what will ensure that implementation is happening and that the company stays on track to achieve its transformational goals.

To conclude, I believe Creating Integrated Value, or CIV, is an important evolution of the corporate responsibility and sustainability movement. It combines many of the ideas and practices already in circulation, but signals some important shifts, especially by using the language of integration and value creation. These are concepts that business understands and can even get excited about (whereas CSR and sustainability tend to be put into peripheral boxes, both in people's heads and in companies themselves).

More critical than the new label or the new language is that Integrated Value is most concerned with implementation. It is a methodology for turning the proliferation of societal aspirations and stakeholder expectations into a credible corporate response, without undermining the viability of the business. On the contrary, CIV aims to be a tool for innovation and transformation, which will be essential if business is to become part of the solution to our global challenges, rather than part of the problem.

The limits of business rationalism

So far in this chapter, we've looked at integration in a very pragmatic way. However, another more philosophical way to look at integrated value is to see it as anything that transforms the dying metaphor of business as a "rational machine" into a new metaphor: business as a "living whole".

This idea arose out of one of my business lectures at university many years ago in which Peters and Waterman's famed bestseller, *In Search of Excellence*, was under discussion. As it happened, I was concurrently reading Jan Smuts' scientific and philosophic treatise, *Holism and Evolution* (1926), and was struck by the conceptual parallels between the "rational mode" of business which Waterman and Peters (1985) were criticizing and the restrictive "mechanism" which Smuts attributed to the scientific community of the 1920s. Since Smuts (1926) regarded his theory of holism as the "necessary antidote to the analytical methods which prevailed", I began to wonder about its remedial potential for the ailing business theory of the present day.

So how might holism might be applied as a new framework for thinking about integrated value in business?

Smuts' starting point in the 1920s was his conviction that the prevailing view of science was both outdated and limiting. He was referring, of course, to the commonly held believe that the universe was "a system or combination whose action can be mathematically calculated from those of its component parts". In more simple terms, it was Newton's concept of the clockwork universe where, "when isolated elements or factors of the complex situation have been separately studied, they are recombined in order to reconstitute the original situation".

Smuts' (1926) main criticism of this reductionist view of reality, which he called "mechanism", centred on its failure to recognize the countless synergies which exist in the world around and within us, as well as its inability to account for the process of creative evolution. In his own words, it was:

> a fixed dogma, that there could be no more in the effect than there was in the cause; hence creativity and real progress became impossible … In its analytical pursuit of the part, science had missed the whole, and thus tended to reduce the world to dead aggregations rather than to the real living wholes which make up nature.

Smuts' (1926) belief was that "in studying and interpreting Nature, we need to be faithful to our experience of her", and that "our experience is largely fluid and plastic, with little that is rigid and much that is indefinite about it". His recommendation was that "we should as far as possible withstand the temptation to pour this plastic experience into the moulds of our hard and narrow preconceived notions".

This diagnosis by Smuts of the malaise infecting science of the 1920s bears striking resemblance, we find, to the critique by Waterman and Peters (1985) of the "rationalist view" which has dominated business thinking since the 1980s. In a sense, this is not surprising, given that both stem from what management authority Peter Drucker (1959) calls "the Cartesian world-view", after Rene Descartes' early 17th-century vision of the universe as a grand machine, which Drucker discusses in his book, *The Landmarks of Tomorrow* (Drucker, 1959).

The application of this concept to business owes its theoretical foundations to American engineer, Frederick Taylor, and German sociologist, Max Weber, who, towards the end of the 1800s, introduced their ideas of scientific management and bureaucratic organization respectively. These were subsequently enshrined by the likes of Ford Motor Company and others in the 20th century, and in many cases taken to an extreme following the explosive growth of the high-tech industry. The classic production line is a case in point.

We find, therefore, a dominant philosophy of business which could be described as "management by numbers" and which includes the following popular notions: success in terms of short-term profitability, growth, and return to financial shareholders; rational decision-making supported by quantitative analysis; increased productivity through measurements, controls and monetary incentives; and organizations and communication in the form of hierarchies.

Waterman and Peter's criticism of this rationalistic view of business concerns its lack of appreciation for the qualitative dimensions of management, as well as its limited understanding of the complexity of the human being. As I quoted before (but it's worth restating):

> The problem with the rationalist view of organizing people is that people are not very rational. To fit Taylor's old model, or today's organizational charts, man is simply designed wrong (or of course, vice versa, according to our argument here). In fact, if our understanding of the current state of psychology is even close to correct, man is the ultimate study in conflict and paradox.

Creating integrated value through holism

Given the similarity between the old models described above, it is my conviction that Smuts has some important insights to offer in the search for a new, more integral vision of business. These are to be found in his theory of holism which I shall attempt to summarize.

In essence, holism (from the Greek *holos*, meaning "whole") involved a synthesis between Darwin's theory of evolution (1856), Einstein's theory of relativity (1905) and Smuts' (1926) own reflections on the evolution of matter, life and mind. The result was a revolutionary concept with far-reaching implications. What Smuts (1926) claimed to have identified was nothing less than "the ultimate synthetic, ordering, organizing, regulative activity in the universe, which accounts for all the structural groupings and syntheses in it".

At the heart of this idea is Smuts' concept of "wholes" which he believed to be "the real units of nature". He describes their character as "a unity of parts which is so close and intense as to become more than the sum of its parts" (that is, they are synergistic). He goes on to say that:

> every organism, every plant or animal, is a whole, with a certain internal organisation and measure of self direction, and an individual specific character of its own. This is true of the lowest micro-organism no less than the most highly developed and complex human personality.

Implicit in this concept of wholes, Smuts (1926) argues, is also the principle of evolution: "There is a creative activity, progress and development of wholes, and the successive phases of this creative evolution are marked by the development of ever more complex and significant wholes."

Describing the process in more detail, he says:

> At the start the fact of the structure is all-important in wholes, but as we ascend the scale of wholes, we see structure becoming secondary to function, we see function becoming the dominant feature of the whole, we see it as a correlation of all the activities of the structure and affecting new syntheses which are more and more of a creative character.

It is in this sense that he refers to mechanism as simply "an earlier, cruder form of holism".

The question is: can these rather philosophical and scientific concepts be applied to business?

Well, as it happens, Smuts (1926) repeatedly implied that such an application would not be inappropriate. "What is not generally recognized," he wrote, "is that the conception of wholes applies in a sense to human associations like the State, and to the creations of the human spirit in all its greatest and most significant activities."

It is to business as a specific form of "human association" that I now turn in order to apply holism as a new paradigm.

Recognizing the integrated manager

The first level of business to which a holistic view needs to be applied is that of the individual. As previously implied, the old view of business regards employees as rational entities who are expected to perform in mechanical ways to further the materialistic goals of the company. In contrast, Smuts' views of the human being, as expressed through personality, was as "the highest and completest of all wholes". It is interesting now to note that, while this idea has yet to be fully applied in business, the idea itself is not new to the discipline.

In fact, thinking along these lines began to emerge in the 1930s, following Elton Mayo's now famed Hawthorne experiments, which showed the importance of psychological factors in employee behaviour. Building on this, Douglas McGregor, in *The Human Side of Enterprise* (McGregor, 1960), challenged the idea that "authority is the central, indispensable means of managerial control" by introducing his Theory Y of motivation. Then Abraham Maslow (1954), in *Motivation and Personality*, made his invaluable contribution in the form of his hierarchy of needs, which, incidentally, later led him to the concept of *Eupsychian Management* (Maslow, 1965), in which the "being values" of his hierarchy of needs (such as self-actualization) were more explicitly recognized.

Another significant development, previously mentioned, which should have advanced the recognition of the whole individual, occurred in the 1960s and 1970s when 25 patients around the world underwent "split-brain" surgery for the treatment of severe epilepsy. The unexpected results showed that the brain's right and left hemispheres can operate independently and display significantly different characteristics, the left-brain controlling essentially rational and reductionist activity, and the right-brain performing more of an integrative and creative function. Canadian business researcher, Henry Mintzberg (1976), was the first to spot the business application and explained its significance in his article in *Harvard Business Review* called "Planning on the Left Side and Managing the Right", saying:

> One fact recurs repeatedly in all of this (management) research: the key managerial processes are enormously complex and mysterious, drawing on the vaguest of information and using the least articulated of mental processes. These processes seem to be more relational and holistic than ordered and sequential, and more intuitive than intellectual; they seem to be most characteristic of right-hemispheric activity.

The point is that, despite all the evidence and frameworks supporting the notion of the holistic individual, business has yet to respond in a meaningful way. Employees are still regarded by companies as inputs to production and expenses in business rather than creative beings and assets in business. People are still expected to leave their emotions, intuition, dreams, fears, family and community concerns, and a myriad other qualities characteristic of being fully human, outside of the workplace. And as workers, they are still expected to be motivated and inspired by monetary incentives, increased productivity and profit-making, as opposed to personal development, genuine service to others, and the search for meaning in their lives. The time is long overdue for business to being to serve humans rather than the other way around.

The new law of the market: survival of the "wholest"

The other level to which holistic thinking can be applied is that of the organization. For instance, does Smuts' idea of mechanism being "an earlier, cruder form of Holism" not also apply to business? After all, it is indeed as a result of increasing complexity (as per its original meaning of an increase in interconnections or relationships) that the rational model of organization is no longer working. This theme has, in fact, already been pursued by Dutch psychiatrist, Bernard Lievegoed, in *Managing the Developing Organization* (Lievegoed, 1991), in which he conceives of the development of organizations through three phases: the pioneering phase, the phase of differentiation (the rational model) and the phase of integration (the holistic model).

Inherent in the new holistic organization is the idea of flattening the hierarchy, and a move towards the network-type organization which recognizes its composite wholes more fully. The team-based culture, as well as organizing according to process (as opposed to functional silos), is also part of the move towards a more holistic structure and is more consistent with Smuts' notion of synergy than its mechanistic predecessor. This thinking needs to be extended beyond the internal organization.

Another interesting derivative from Smuts' (1926) holism could be his concept of "fields" of influence, which he describes as the "natural shading-off continuities" of wholes as opposed to "enclosing things or people in hard contours which are purely artificial". This separation is exactly what business has been guilty of in the past, both with regards to its people (as highlighted in the previous section) and its relationship to its external environment. Indeed, it is only recently that business is beginning to think in terms of its responsibility to all its stakeholders, as opposed to simply its managers and financial shareholders. And even so, much of this remains superficial and inadequate, as in the case of the destruction of the natural environment.

Paul Hawken, author of *The Ecology of Commerce* (Hawken, 1993), makes this point with regard to the latter: "If every company on the planet were to adopt the best environmental practice of the 'leading' companies, the world would still be moving toward sure degradation and collapse." The reason, says Hawken, is that "rather than a management problem, we have a design problem, a flaw that runs through all business". And "to create an enduring society" business will be required to create a "system of commerce and production where every act is inherently sustainable and restorative".

Ryuzaburo Kaku, Japanese chairman of the Canon group of companies, is perhaps one of the few who has taken this holistic understanding to its natural conclusion in thinking about business. He explains that, in the highest stage of evolution of a corporation, "a global consciousness emerges and the corporation sees itself contributing to the whole of mankind". This evolutionary perspective is important in applying Smuts' (1926) holism to business. It highlights the need for what Peter Senge (2006), professor of Systems Thinking at MIT's Business School, calls, in *The Fifth Discipline*, the creation of the "learning organization". In fact, Senge's systems thinking is nothing other than a subsequent iteration of the principles of holism.

In Smuts' terms, the message is the same, for while the tendency in the universe is towards higher and more complex wholes, degeneration also occurs when "there are wholes that are weak, inchoate, and these must be eliminated". Therefore, those organizations least able to transform themselves continually into more and more holistic entities will be those which have failed to adapt and will die. It is after all, according to Smuts (1926), the fundamental law of the universe: survival of the "wholest".

The quest for meaning as the ultimate integrated value

Extending the idea of integration, surprisingly little has been written about the integration between corporate sustainability and responsibility (CSR) and the search for meaning in the workplace. It is surprising partly because meaning has been a serious topic of research and application for at least 50 years now, following the seminal work of psychiatrist Viktor Frankl and others, as have the fields of industrial psychology and CSR. But it is more surprising still simply because work is where we spend about a third of our lives. If meaning cannot be found in the workplace, our ability to lead a fulfilling life is seriously impaired.

The importance of understanding how work can contribute to meaning in life seems more critical now than ever before. Anecdotal evidence is mounting that people in the West are increasingly feeling a sense of existential crisis in their working lives. On the one hand, they are expecting more from their work experience, including that it will nurture personal development and self-actualization. On the other hand, they are finding the capitalist, corporate model of work to be lacking in a meaningful higher purpose, or to put it another way, the modern workplace and economy is devoid of a sense of soul.

Some may argue that this growing frustration in the Western workplace is a vindication of Karl Marx's concept of the "alienation of labour" through capitalism, whereby work:

> does not belong to his essential being; that he therefore does not confirm himself in his work, but denies himself, feels miserable and not happy, does not develop free mental and physical energy, but mortifies his flesh and ruins his mind.

Modern social commentators such as Charles Handy are less extreme, arguing for reformation rather than revolution. In his book, *The Hungry Spirit* (Handy, 1998), which is subtitled "Beyond Capitalism: A Quest for Purpose in the Modern World", Handy calls for capitalism to embrace the notion of social capital (and I would add ecological capital as well) in addition to the more traditional economic capital. He also emphasizes the need for citizen companies, which demonstrate greater accountability and a restored balance between the rights and responsibilities of business.

The question remains, however, whether these ideas have any grounding in the theory of meaning on the one hand, and management theory on the other hand. According to Frankl's (2006) logopsychology and logophilosophy, work—doing, or as he referred to it, realizing creative values—constitutes one of three paths to meaning. "As long as creative values are in the forefront of the life task," he noted, "their actualisation generally coincides with a person's work." In fact, his other two paths to meaning may be equally applicable in the work situation, even if less common, namely being, or the experience of values (e.g. love, truth, beauty), and perceiving, or the adoption of constructive attitudes (especially in the face of suffering).

Frankl's notions of work as ideally being an expression of a life task are not dissimilar to iconic industrial psychologist Abraham Maslow's (1971) conclusions about self-actualizing individuals. Writing about the higher-order needs of his famous motivational hierarchy, Maslow (1971) used words such as "vocation", "calling", "mission", "duty", "beloved job", even "oblation", to describe the sense of dedication and devotion to their work experienced by self-actualizing people. Maslow (1971) interestingly also identified high levels of perceived meaningfulness in the lives of the self-actualizing subjects that he studied.

This was not the only similarity between their conceptions of work and meaning. Both Frankl (2006) and Maslow (1971) qualify their comments by emphasizing that work only becomes meaningful when it entails contribution to a cause, or society, beyond selfish needs. Maslow (1971) talks about "offering oneself or dedicating oneself upon some altar for some particular task, some cause outside oneself and bigger than oneself, something not merely selfish" and Frankl (2006) introduces his concept of responsibility by saying that "this meaning and value is attached to the person's work as a contribution to society, not to the actual occupation as such".

Only Oliver Philips (1979) appears to have attempted any substantive conceptual application of the Frankl's theory of meaning to business. In a chapter entitled "A New Course for Management", he proposes a model in which the human will to meaning can be channelled in one of three directions in organizations. It can either find healthy expression in freedom of choice with responsibility (leading to self-transcendence and unique meaning), or it can be frustrated by a lack of freedom and responsibility (leading to collective neurosis and nihilism), or there can be a failure to find meaning (leading to existential frustration and reductionism).

Key influencing factors, according to Philips (1979), are management style (authoritarian companies make successful meaning-seeking difficult), strategic horizon (focus on profits encourages short-term thinking which detracts from meaning) and job enrichment (categorizing and depersonalizing jobs makes them less meaningful). He builds on Frankl and Maslow's ideas of self-transcendence, saying that in affluent societies, "dedication to something outside one's self-interest is stronger motivation to work than money or power" and a person will therefore "look for new meaning potentials in work that benefits his co-workers, minority groups he identifies with and causes he considers worth supporting". This begins to hint at the link between work, meaning and social responsibility.

In perhaps the strongest theoretical support of this link, academic Paul Wong's Personal Meaning Profile model identifies "self-transcendence" as one of seven factors that characterizes people's perceptions about what makes an ideally meaningful life. Some of the descriptive statements associated with this factor make its relevance clear, for example: I believe I can make a difference in the world; I strive to make the world a better place; it is important to dedicate my life to a cause; I make a significant contribution to society; and I attempt to leave behind a good and lasting legacy.

Hence, one of the ways companies can address an apparent lack of purpose and meaning in the workplace, which may in turn be associated with lower levels of employee motivation, job satisfaction and worker loyalty, is to actively engage in corporate sustainability and social responsibility activities. By the same token, employees that make an effort to be involved in these initiatives in their workplace, be it through volunteering on community projects or in other ways, are likely to experience an enhanced their sense of meaning in the lives. This then—the integration of work, purpose and sustainability—may be the final piece in the puzzle of created integrated value in and through business.

8
Unlocking change through future-fitness

A test for future-fitness

Are you fit for the future? Will your product, organization, community, city or country survive and thrive in 10, 20, 50 or even 100 years?

We live in a world that is changing faster and challenging us more than ever before. Great progress has been made in lifting people out of poverty, advancing scientific frontiers, connecting the globe with technology and making knowledge more accessible. At the same time, there are disturbing trends of increasing inequality, catastrophic destruction of ecosystems and loss of species, pervasive corruption, increasingly volatile and dangerous climate change, waves of forced migration and floods of refugees, a rise of religious extremism and the omnipresent threat of terrorism.

The question is: How can we—as individuals, businesses, communities and policy-makers—prepare for the future? How can we maximize our chances of success, not only by being ready, but also by helping to shape the future that we desire? I think it helps to view future-fitness in two ways: in terms of alignment—i.e. fitting, like a jigsaw piece, into the bigger picture of an emerging world; and in terms of agility—i.e. building up the kind of fitness that allows quick reflexes and strong performance in response to future conditions.

The biggest trends in society and our most enduring ideals suggest that there are five key criteria for future-fitness: our products, organizations, communities, cities or countries must be safe, smart, shared, sustainable

Criteria	Test question	Keywords	Example indicators
Safe	Does this product, organization, community, city or country protect and care for us?	Healthy, secure, resilient	OH&S, toxicity, risk and emergency preparedness
Smart	Does this product, organization, community, city or country connect and empower us?	Educated, connected, responsive	Connectivity, access to knowledge, R&D investment
Shared	Does this product, organization, community, city or country include and value us?	Fair, diverse, inclusive	Value distribution, stakeholder participation, diversity
Sustainable	Does this product, organization, community, city or country protect and restore our environment?	Renewable, enduring, evolutionary	Externality pricing, footprint analysis, renewability
Satisfying	Does this product, organization, community, city or country fulfil and inspire us?	Beneficial, beautiful, meaningful	Quality standards, levels of satisfaction, happiness

TABLE 6   The Kaleidoscope Five-S Future-Fitness Framework

and satisfying? I call these the "Five Ss of Future-Fitness", which are summarized in Table 6 and then briefly described.

These visions of the future can help to guide our actions in the present. As the Cheshire Cat so wisely put it in Lewis Carroll's *Alice's Adventures in Wonderland*, "If you don't know where you're going, any road will get you there" (Carroll, 1865). So, according to the Five Ss, where are we going?

- A **safe** future is one in which our products, organizations, communities, cities and countries do not damage our health and wellbeing; rather, they minimize our exposure to toxins, sickness, disease and danger, allowing us to feel physically and psychologically secure. Examples include the Zero Toxics campaign in the textiles industry, GE's Healthymagination programme, Freeplay's off-grid foetal heart-rate monitor and HP's Global Social Innovation in Health programme.

- A **smart** future is one in which our products, organizations, communities, cities and countries use technology to connect us to each other more effectively and allow us to share what we value most. They also facilitate more democratic governance by allowing us (as customers or citizens) to give direct, immediate feedback. Examples include IBM's Smarter Planet initiative, Karmayog's online corruption reporting system, Wikirate, A Little World and the World Wide Web Foundation's Web Index.

- A **shared** future is one in which our products, organizations, communities, cities and countries address issues of equity and access by being transparent about the distribution of value in society and working to ensure that benefits are fairly shared and diversity is respected. Examples include GSK's patent pool, the GreenXchange, Kickstarter's crowdfunding site, the Fairtrade Foundation, the e-Choupal farmer empowerment digital scheme and the Occupy movement.

- A **sustainable** future is one in which our products, organizations, communities, cities and countries begin to operate within the limits of the planet by radically changing resource consumption patterns and ecosystem impacts. This includes a shift to renewable energy and resources, closing the loop on production and moving to a low-carbon society. Examples include Interface's Mission Zero, Unilever's Sustainable Living Plan, energy-surplus houses and Cradle to Cradle certified companies.

- A **satisfying** future is one in which our products, organizations, communities, cities and countries produce high-quality services that satisfy our human needs, as well as enabling a lifestyle and culture that values quality of life, happiness and other indicators of wellbeing. Examples include Six Sigma quality systems, B Corps (for benefit corporations), GoodGuide's product rating system, New Economics Foundation's Happy Planet Index, and the Slow Food and Downshifting movements.

The way to apply future-fitness thinking is to test the anticipated stocks and flows in society against these five criteria. For example, do the projected stocks of nature, infrastructure, institutions, people and capital suggest that our product, organization, community, city or country will be more (or less) safe, smart, shared, sustainable and satisfying? Likewise, do the expected flows of materials, energy, knowledge, money and products suggest a future that is more (or less) healthy, inclusive, connected, renewable and fulfilling?

In the final analysis, our hope for the future is based on creating a better world tomorrow than we have today; a society that gives more freedom and fulfilment to our children and grandchildren than we have enjoyed. The Kaleidoscope Five-S Future-Fitness Framework is just one way to crystallize what a better future could look like—and to galvanize our efforts in shaping the products, organizations, communities, cities and countries that could turn such a bright vision into reality.

How Web 2.0 is shaping the future of business

The Five Ss are by no means mutually exclusive. On the contrary, the represent a complex set of overlapping and interweaving dynamics. For example, we are seeing how movement towards a Smart future can have also help to create a more Sustainable future. Let's explore this synergy a bit further. How is the Web 2.0 revolution shaping the sustainability agenda?

Wikipedia defines Web 2.0 as "web applications that facilitate interactive information sharing, interoperability, user-centred design and collaboration". The term owes its origins to a 1999 article by IT consultant Darcy DiNucci, which challenged programmers to adapt to the spread of portable Web-ready devices.

The concept was broadened out in 2005 by online media pioneer Tim O'Reilly, who contrasted Web 1.0 and Web 2.0 using as examples DoubleClick versus Google AdSense, Britannica Online versus Wikipedia, personal websites versus blogging, publishing versus participation, directories (taxonomy) versus tagging (folksonomy) and stickiness versus syndication, to mention but a few.

In 2006, Don Tapscott and Anthony Williams showed how Web 2.0 was set to disrupt how markets operate and how businesses are organized. They called this new paradigm *Wikinomics* (Tapscott and Williams, 2007), defining it as "the effects of extensive collaboration and user-participation on the marketplace and corporate world".

Wikinomics, they said, is based on four principles:

1. **Openness**, which includes not only open standards and content but also financial transparency and an open attitude towards external ideas and resources.

2. **Peering**, which replaces hierarchical models with a more collaborative forum, for which the Linux operating system is a quintessential example.

3. **Sharing**, which is a less proprietary approach to (among other things) products, intellectual property, bandwidth and scientific knowledge.

4. **Acting globally**, which involves embracing globalization and ignoring physical and geographical boundaries at both the corporate and individual level.

Another Web 2.0 building block is Chris Anderson's concept of *The Long Tail* (Anderson, 2006)—named after the area of a statistical distribution curve where it approaches (but never quite meets) the axis. Anderson's breakthrough idea was that, in a Web 2.0 era, selling less to more people is big business. The Long Tail questions the conventional wisdom that says success is about generating "blockbusters" and "superstars"—those rare few products and services that become runaway bestsellers.

Anderson (2006) sums up his message by saying that:

- The Long Tail of available variety is longer than we think.

- It's now within reach economically.

- All those niches, when aggregated, can make up a significant market.

- The Long Tail revolution has been made possible by the digital age, which has dramatically reduced the costs of customized production and niche distribution.

Through the Web 2.0 lens of Tapscott and Williams' (2007) four principles (openness, peering, sharing and acting globally), plus another principle derived from Anderson's "long tail" concept (mass customization), let's take a look at the sustainable future of business.

Net value footprinting and forensic impact analysis

Net value footprinting

Business has evolved over the past two decades from being highly opaque to gradually embracing a more transparent disclosure practices. This has been a result of regulation (such as the Toxic Release Inventory in the US, which requires thousands of American companies to report over 650 toxic chemicals) and voluntary efforts (such as the GRI, which is now developing the fourth iteration of is Sustainability Reporting Guidelines).

In a Web 2.0 world, however, transparency requirements are taken to another level. Companies are expected to go beyond GRI-based reporting, to measure and disclose the their impacts across the entire product life-cycle or value chain. This process of quantifying business's economic, social and environmental costs to society is sometimes called full-cost accounting, or internalizing externalities. I call it Net Value Footprinting.

Net Value Footprinting is being pioneered by the likes of Patagonia (with their Footprint Chronicles™), Puma (with their Environmental Profit and Loss statement), The Economics of Ecosystems and Biodiversity (TEEB) study, and the Global Footprint Network.

Forensic impact analysis

While progressive companies are steadily improving their transparency, there will also be millions of irresponsible companies that try to fly under the radar of regulation and public scrutiny. In an effort to be lowest cost producers or preferred suppliers to big brand multinationals, they will deliberately externalize social and environmental costs by running polluting operations that exploit cheap labour and abuse human rights.

But in a Web 2.0 world, these rogue businesses will be caught and exposed through the emerging practice of what I call Forensic Impact Analysis. This will happen through a combination of traceability technology (which finds the electronic footprints left by all businesses in the supply chain), forensic substance analysis (which can identify the source of fibres, chemicals and other product components) and vigilant activists and consumers (who will capture malpractices on mobile phones using photographs, videos and audio recordings, and leak these via online social media).

Forensic Impact Analysis is being pioneered by the food industry, which uses bar codes or RFID tags and other tracking media to monitor every step of their production process (GrapeNet in India is an example). Other examples include Karmayog (which allows online whistle-blowing on corruption in India) and WikiLeaks (which exposed Trafigura's dumping of toxic waste along the Ivory Coast).

Stakeholder crowdsourcing and disruptive partnerships

Stakeholder crowdsourcing

Companies from the Web 1.0 era still believe that focus groups, public meetings, stakeholder panels and the occasional online or in-store survey are adequate for taking the pulse of their stakeholders. At the same time, they are generally distrustful of ideas or solutions from outside their organizations. In short, they suffer from the "not invented here" syndrome.

By contrast, Web 2.0-savvy companies realize that the world has moved into an era of crowdsourcing—as previously discussed, a term coined by Jeff Howe in 2006 and closely linked to the earlier idea of "wisdom of crowds" popularized by James Surowiecki. Turning this concept into practice, future business will increasingly use filtered, "expert crowds" to monitor their reputation, get feedback on sustainable products innovations and solicit help in solving difficult ethical dilemmas.

Stakeholder crowdsourcing is being pioneered by companies such as Sony, through its two online campaigns, Open Planet Ideas and FutureScapes (to generate new sustainable technology ideas) and platforms such as Convetit, which General Electric has used to crowdsource feedback on its sustainability communications.

Disruptive partnerships

Companies have had a decade to get used to the idea of cross-sector partnerships, which have been heavily promoted through the United Nations and given a boost through inclusion in the Millennium Development Goals.

In a Web 2.0 world, however, business is expected to get into more challenging partnerships—collaborations which disrupt the status quo. For example, Greenpeace very effectively used social media to campaign against Nestlé's Kit Kat brand, after finding an Indonesian supplier that was clearing tropical rainforest to grow palm oil. A year later, Greenpeace praised Nestlé for their "no deforestation" commitment through its challenging partnership with TFT, a sustainable forestry NGO.

Disruptive Partnerships are being pioneered by the likes of Rio Tinto (partnering with the World Conservation Union to reduce their biodiversity impacts), BASF (through their Strategic Alliance for the Fortification of Oil and Other Staple Foods partnership with GIZ), and Netherlands flooring company Desso (using their Circle of Architects creative forum).

Open sourcing and wiki-ratings

Open sourcing

One of the biggest changes in the society over the past ten years has been the explosion of social media. But this revolution goes beyond sharing our holiday photos on Facebook or microblogging the minutiae of our lives on

Twitter. The more fundamental innovation is a shift in thinking and practice towards "open sourcing", which at its heart is about co-creation.

Let's look at an example from the pharmaceutical industry to illustrate the point. After a decade under siege—with Big Pharma being accused of overpricing their patented brands and blocking access to cheaper generic (and often life-saving) drugs—GlaxoSmithKline (GSK)'s CEO Andrew Witty committed GSK to put any chemicals or processes over which it has intellectual property rights that are relevant to finding drugs for neglected diseases into a "patent pool", so they can be explored by other researchers.

Other pioneering examples include the World Business Council for Sustainable Development's (WBCSD) Eco-Patent Commons and the Creative Commons' GreenXchange, both of which allow companies to share their intellectual property "for the common good", especially on issues such as waste, pollution, climate change and energy. Tesla Motors also open sourced its electric car patents in 2014.

Wiki-ratings

Another feature of Web 2.0 design is that it easily allows users to express an opinion on others' content—from the ubiquitous thumbs-up "Like" feature on Facebook, to the fresh-red versus rotten-green tomato movie rating system on rottentomatoes.com.

Now, we are going beyond these simplistic approaches to dynamic, wiki-based platforms that allow the public to rate—and comment in detail—on the economic, governance, social and environmental performance of companies. One such innovative platform, which I have been directly involved in, is Wikirate, founded by Philipp Hirche. Not only does Wikirate use a crowdsourcing approach to ratings, but in much the same way as Wikipedia, it allows for real-time updating. Hence, an ethical infringement, or a sustainability innovation, will be reflected almost immediately in the company's wikirating.

Other pioneering examples in the ratings space are GoodGuide, WeGreen, Project Label and Scryve, although judging by SustainAbility's Rate the Raters report, none of the 108 rating systems identified employ a methodology quite so democratic and transparent as Wikirate.

Prototyping and smart mobbing

Prototyping

Innovation has always used prototyping—i.e. designing a working sample of new products and services. The difference in a Web 2.0 world is that prototypes are launched early, as imperfect versions, to solicit rapid user feedback in a process often called "beta testing".

One way to bring about such rapid, open source prototyping is through competitions. Take the X-Prize, for example, which describes its mission as "bringing about radical breakthroughs for the benefit of humanity" in five areas: education, global development, energy and environment, life sciences, and exploration. Through this platform, multimillion-dollar prizes are offered for innovative solutions in everything from "progressive automotive" and "oil clean-up" to "health sensors" and "diagnostic technologies".

Another pioneering example is Virgin's $25 million Earth Challenge, for "a commercially viable design which results in the net removal of anthropogenic, atmospheric greenhouse gases so as to contribute materially to the stability of the Earth's climate system".

Smart mobbing

Web 2.0 technologies have spawned a new type of protest activity, called smart mobbing. This simply means using real-time media and sharing platforms—especially SMS texts and status updates (such as tweets on Twitter)—to rapidly organize a crowd.

Examples include viral text messaging in the Philippines that helped to oust former President Joseph Estrada in 2001 and the use of Twitter during the Arab Spring uprisings in 2011. Smart mobs can also co-ordinate virtual activity, such as when the "hacktivist" group Anonymous encouraged its followers to launch cyber attacks against Visa, MasterCard, PayPal and other companies opposing WikiLeaks in 2011. Similarly, Greenpeace encouraged smart mobbing following its 2010 campaign against Nestlé's Kit Kat brand. The campaign video was viewed by half a million people in four days, and unleashed a flood of angry comments on Nestlé's Facebook page.

Smart mobbing can also be used positively, such as when "Mission 4636" created an SMS text mapping emergency communications system after the 2010 Haiti earthquake. In future, companies and governments will increasingly need to anticipate and respond to activist smart mobs, as well as seeding their own.

App farming and plug-and-play

App farming

Despite some great new gadgets over the past few years—such as tablets or wearable tech—the war of the computing giants has turned into a "battle of apps". Underlying this explosive trend, by July 2014, Android users were able to choose between 1.3 million apps on the Google Play platform, while Apple's App Store remained the second-largest app store with 1.2 million available apps.

Apps (software applications) are essentially neatly packaged, user-friendly online services, ranging from games (e.g. Angry Birds, Scrabble) and music (e.g. Spotify, Shazam) to education (e.g. NASA, Spelling Bee) and business (e.g. HBR Tips, EasyMoney 1.0). There is also a new generation of apps focused on social and environmental solutions. Google Play lists more than 400 sustainability-related apps. The most popular is BlaBlaCar, which connects drivers with empty seats with people looking for a ride, allowing users to post on, and search, the biggest European car sharing community.

Other popular apps in this genre include GoodGuide (for ethical shopping), carbon footprint calculators (Google Play lists five) and educational games such as Sustainable Me. Hence, businesses of the future will be judged on whether they can seed and grow farms of apps that provide solutions to the world's most serious challenges.

Plug-and-play

The final Web 2.0-savvy practice is to think in terms of "plug and play" solutions. Essentially, this is a form of smart technology that detects its operating environment, installs whatever software is needed and is operational without any action by the user.

To take a simple example, rather than having to manually unplug or switch off household electrical devices to save energy, a plug-and-play device in the home automatically detects all idle devices and disables them remotely. Similar approaches apply to optimal energy-efficient heating and cooling of buildings (i.e. indoor climate regulation) and low-carbon driving, which automatically chooses the emission-minimizing acceleration and cruise speeds.

Plug-and-play also applies to our shopping preferences. In the future, we will have automatic product filters that match our personal preferences—whether it is for fair trade, organic, beauty without cruelty, or health. When shopping online, we will only see products that match our personal criteria. Similarly, in-store we will be alerted to products that meet our standards—a process achieved through auto-scanning by our mobile devices of in-store bar codes and associated criteria-linked product databases.

The message is clear for business. Web 2.0 is not just about everybody being continuously online. Rather, it is about a business new mind-set that thinks in terms of the collective intelligence of its stakeholders, the co-creation of solutions to our global challenges, and the use of technology to achieve speed and scale in spreading innovation to those parts of the world that have the biggest and most urgent unmet needs.

Future images: beyond the Information Age

As we move further into the future, some argue that Web 2.0 will be super-seded more inspiring and empowering trends. A good place to start is to get the Industrial Age well behind us, for it has been a crumbling image for at least the past four decades. In its wake, however, we find the explosive rise of a revolutionary successor. I am of course referring to the Information Age. Notable authors on this subject include Peter Drucker, Robert Theobald, Daniel Bell, Yoneji Masuda, John Naisbitt, Alvin Toffler and Peter Russell.

Few people today would disagree that the Information Age represents the popular metaphor of our time. However, the question for the future is, does this fashionable image have the energy and endurance to carry humanity into the 21st century and beyond? In reply, many say: "Yes, for it has yet to fully transform society", and they cite visions of an emerging global soci-ety, decentralized, yet intimately linked by the wonders of information technology. Others, though less prescriptive and fewer in number, say: "No, society is already reaching beyond the Information Age and a new vision is needed which will help clarify and call forth the next phase of our collective development."

One of the pioneering voices in this regard is American futurist Hazel Henderson. In her book *Paradigms in Progress* (Henderson, 1993), she states her position unequivocally:

> The Information Age is no longer an adequate image for the present, let alone a guide to the future. It still focuses on hardware technolo-gies, mass production and economic models of efficiency and compe-tition, and is more an extension of industrial ideas and methods than a new stage in human development.

Henderson's (1993) suggested alternative is what she calls a "re-patterning of the exploding Information Age" into an emerging new "Age of Light". She bases this image on evidence of a growing realization by humanity of its dependence on nature, and more precisely, on light from the sun. Beyond the mushrooming ecological movement and the call for sustainable development, she draws support for her theory from the recent phenomenal growth in leading-edge technologies which do nothing more than attempt to mimic the ingenuity of Nature—a phenomenon also well catalogued by Janine Benyus in her book *Biomimicry* (Benyus, 1997). The most obvious examples include:

- **Artificial intelligence technologies**: expert systems, hypertext, associative learning programmes, multiprocessor parallel computers, neural net computers.

- **Biotechnologies**: gene splicing, molecular engineering, cloning, plant hybridization, bio-remediation, immunology, gene machines, nanotechnologies.

- **Energy technologies**: photovoltaic cells, fusion reactors, biomass converters, membrane technologies, molecular assemblers, synthetic photosynthesis.

- **Lightwave technologies (phototronics)**: fibre optics, optical scanners, lasers, holography, optical computers, imaging technologies, solar technologies.

Henderson (1993) explains that her conception of the Age of Light goes even further, however, and suggests that it includes a symbolic interpretation, namely the "flowering of our consciousness in a new Age of Enlightenment". This idea of Henderson's dovetails nicely with the work of Peter Russell, author of the ground-breaking book *The Awakening Earth* (Russell, 1984).

Russell (1984) draws the following conclusions from his research:

> Rapid as the growth of the information industry is, it may still not be the fastest growing area of human activity. There are indications that the movement towards the transformation of consciousness (i.e. self-development and inner growth) is growing even faster. The number of people involved in this area seems to be doubling every four years or so ... If the growth of interest continues to swell, so will the number of people, and we may reach a point, possibly sometime early next century, when the employment curve for "consciousness processing" will overtake that of information processing. The evolution of human

consciousness will then have shifted from the Information Age into the Consciousness Age.

The implications of a transition to the Consciousness Age are outlined by Russell (1984) in a scenario which he calls the High Synergy Society. He describes some of the likely consequences of such a shift in the following terms:

- **No limits to growth**: personal and spiritual growth become as important, if not more important, than growth defined in material terms.

- **Unemployment revalued**: the reduced need for formal employment and a growing use of time for inner development (self-actualization).

- **Healthy, holy and whole**: a movement towards holistic health practices and a corresponding decrease in physiological stress and illness.

- **Left and right**: a shift towards greater synthesis of right-brain (feminine/*yin*) and left-brain (masculine/*yang*) qualities.

- **Synchronicity rules**: an increase in the occurrence of meaningful coincidences at an individual and collective (social superorganism) level.

Certainly positive, transformative visions of the future—beyond the Information Age—are not limited to those of Henderson and Russell. Others may be found in the writings of Marilyn Ferguson (1982) in *The Aquarian Conspiracy*, Fritjof Capra (1982) in *The Turning Point*; Francis Kinsman (1990) in *Millennium*; Willis Harman (1980) in *Global Mind Change* and Jonathon Porritt (2013) in *The World We Made*, to mention but a few. Whatever you favourite metaphor, do not underestimate the importance of identifying and working with these "post-industrial" guiding images and thereby creating a better future for all life on Earth. After all, we do, literally, create our future, limited only by the boundaries of our imagination.

Sustainable frontiers forecasts for the next ten years

So how is the future of sustainable business looking? Let me share ten forecasts, which summarize much of the thinking in this book.

Sustainable frontiers forecast 1

First, I have consistently argued that what is needed—and what is just starting to emerge—is a new approach to sustainable enterprise. I don't mind what you call it, but I have described it as Transformative CSR (Corporate Sustainability and Responsibility), or CSR 2.0. This is a purpose-driven, principle-based approach, in which business seeks to identify and tackle the root causes of our present unsustainability and irresponsibility, typically through innovating business models, revolutionizing their processes, products and services and lobbying for progressive national and international policies.

Hence, over the next ten years, we will see most large, international companies having moved through the first four types or stages of CSR (defensive, charitable, promotional and strategic) and practising, to varying degrees, Transformative CSR, or CSR 2.0.

Sustainable frontiers forecast 2

The problem with the current obsession with CSR codes and standards (including the new ISO 26000 standard) is that it encourages a tick-box approach to CSR. But our social and environmental problems are complex and intractable. They need creative solutions, such as the peel-and-stick solar technology that Stanford University has invented, or The Ocean Cleanup, founded by 19-year old Dutchman Boyan Slat. By deploying Slat's system of long floating arms attached to the sea bed for ten years, it is estimated that almost half of the plastic within the Great Pacific Garbage Patch can be removed.

Hence, over the next ten years, reliance on CSR codes, standards and guidelines such as the UN Global Compact, ISO 14001, SA 8000, etc., will be seen as a necessary but insufficient way to practise CSR. Instead, companies will be judged on how innovative they are in using their products and processes to tackle social and environmental problems.

Sustainable frontiers forecast 3

Another shift which is only just beginning is taking CSR solutions to scale. There is no shortage of charming case studies of laudably responsible and sustainable projects. The problem is that so few of them ever go to scale. We need more examples like Walmart's choice editing: by voluntarily limiting the company to the use of sustainable fish, Walmart forces its customers to do the same. Other examples are Nissan's Leaf model, which is targeting the mass market for electric cars, or Phonebloks, which is promoting a modular approach to mobile phone manufacture, to make electronic waste recycling scalable.

Hence, over the next ten years, self-selecting "ethical consumers" will become less relevant as a force for change. Companies—strongly encouraged by government policies and incentives—will scale up their choice editing, i.e. ceasing to offer "less ethical" product ranges, thus allowing guilt-free shopping.

Sustainable frontiers forecast 4

A trend that will continue to strengthen is the use of cross-sector partnerships. This is in recognition of the fact that the problems we face today are too global, complex and multifaceted for a single institution to solve. One good example is the Corporate Leaders Group on Climate Change, which has systematically and collectively urged UK and EU governments to set bolder climate policies.

Hence, over the next ten years, cross-sector partnerships will be at the heart of all CSR approaches. These will increasingly be defined by business bringing its core competences and skills (rather than just its financial resources) to the party, as DHL does with its logistics capability in helping to distribute life-saving medicines to remote areas.

Sustainable frontiers forecast 5

The idea of "think global, act local" has been in circulation for some decades now, and indeed was given prominence at the original Rio Summit in 1992. However, companies are still learning to practise this balancing act, combining international norms with local contexts, finding local solutions that are culturally appropriate, without forsaking universal principles.

Hence, over the next ten years, companies practising CSR 2.0 will be expected to comply with global best practice principles, such as those in the

UN Global Compact or the Ruggie Human Rights Framework, but simultaneously demonstrate sensitivity to local issues and priorities. An example is mining and metals giant BHP Billiton, which have strong climate change policies globally, as well as malaria prevention programmes in Southern Africa.

Sustainable frontiers forecast 6

A clear failing of our current economic and commercial system is based on a fundamentally flawed design, which acts as if there are no limits on resource consumption or waste disposal. Instead, we need a Cradle to Cradle approach, closing all resource loops and ensuring that products and processes are inherently "good", rather than "less bad", as Shaw Carpets does when taking back its carpets at the end of their useful life and Nike is starting to do with its Considered Design principles.

Hence, over the next ten years, progressive companies will be required to demonstrate full life-cycle management of their products, from cradle-to-cradle. We will see most large companies committing to the goal of zero-waste, carbon-neutral and water-neutral production, with mandated take-back schemes for most products.

Sustainable frontiers forecast 7

The way that we measure and report on social, environmental and ethical performance is changing. As the Global Reporting Initiative, the Carbon Disclosure Project and other standards are strengthened, a consensus on useful metrics is emerging. What is still missing, however, is an agreed set of mandatory metrics, publicly accessible in a database, which makes comparison possible. Current CSR indexes rank the same large companies over and over, often with differing conclusions.

Hence, over the next ten years, much like the Generally Accepted Accounting Practices (GAAP), some form of Generally Accepted Sustainability Practices (GASP) will be agreed, including consensus principles, methods, approaches and rules for measuring and disclosing CSR. Furthermore, a set of credible CSR rating agencies will have emerged.

Sustainable frontiers forecast 8

The role of government in the future will still be crucial. Many of the issues that CSR is currently trying to tackle on a voluntary basis will be mandatory in the future, especially with regards to emission reductions (toxins and greenhouse gases), waste practices and transparency. There will also be a gradual harmonization of country-level legislation on social, environmental and ethical issues.

Hence, over the next ten years, many of today's CSR practices will be mandatory requirements. However, CSR will remain a voluntary practice—an innovation and differentiation frontier—for those companies that are either willing and able, or pushed and prodded through non-governmental means, to go ahead of the legislation to improve quality of life around the world.

Sustainable frontiers forecast 9

The form and media for transparency are rapidly evolving, as we have seen. We can expect annual CSR reporting to be increasingly replaced by online, real-time CSR performance data flows. Feeding into these live communications will be Web 2.0 connected social networks and wiki-style forums for crowdsourcing, such as Wikirate and Convetit.

Hence, over the next ten years, corporate transparency will take form of publicly available sets of mandatory disclosed social, environmental and governance data—available down to a product life-cycle impact level—as well as Web 2.0 collaborative CSR feedback platforms, WikiLeaks-type whistle-blowing sites and product rating applications (such as the GoodGuide iPhone app).

Sustainable frontiers forecast 10

The way that companies manage CSR will also change. CSR departments will most likely shrink, disappear or disperse, as the role for a CSR generalist is confined to small policy functions. By contrast, more specialists in various aspects of CSR will be required and performance across responsibility and sustainability dimensions will increasingly be built into corporate performance appraisal systems (salaries, bonuses, promotion opportunities, etc.), as is already the case in companies such as Arcor, the confectionery company in Argentina.

Hence, over the next ten years, CSR will have diversified back into its specialist disciplines and functions, leaving little or no CSR departments behind, yet having more specialists in particular areas (climate, biodiversity, human rights, community involvement, etc.), and more employees with knowledge of how to integrate CSR issues into their functional areas (HR, marketing, finance, etc.).

Collectively, these forecasts reflect a scenario of widespread adoption of CSR 2.0 over the next ten years, a future in which companies become a significant part of the solution to our sustainability crisis, rather than complicit contributors to the problem, as they are today. Given the current global crises and mounting system pressures, and knowing business's ability to adapt and rapidly change, I regard this as a highly likely prediction sketched out by a concerned pragmatist, rather than the wish-list of a CSR "true believer".

To survive in a volatile world businesses must build in resilience

Speaking of "true believers", if you have landed on this page wearing your superhero outfit—and I admit, I may be partly to blame—I'm going to have to ask you to remove your mask, cape and tights now. Don't get me wrong, when the world needs saving and I'm done paying off my mortgage and carrying out the trash, I'll be the first one to dial-a-superhero. But in the meantime …

You see, despite all the visions and forecasts I have shared in this chapter, the world has this nasty habit of changing without our permission; in fact, without us having so much as poked it in the eye. And so we—as individuals, organizations or whole nations—often find that we are no longer the agents of change, but rather its victims. Change happens! And we are left somewhere between mildly irritated and battling for our very survival.

According to *Business Week*, the average life expectancy of a Fortune 500 company is between 40 and 50 years. One third of the Fortune 500 companies in existence in 1970 had vanished by 1983—acquired, merged, or broken to pieces. Looking across the full spectrum of companies, large and small, the average life of companies may be as low as 12.5 years.

So I want to end this chapter will a reality check. Can we really afford to talk about long-term sustainability, when short-term survival is so hard to achieve? The sobering fact is that we face a future in which saving the world may have to wait, while we save ourselves first. Chances are, we will even have to give up the smooth and swanky practice of sustainability, while we get down and dirty in the trenches of rough, rude resilience.

The bad news is that our silky green spandex outfits are probably not going to survive the trip. The good news is that resilience can be learned and planned for in advance. In a world of increasingly volatile sustainability challenges, there are five strategies for resilience that can dramatically increase our chances of survival when the waves of disruptive change come crashing in. They are to: defend, diversify, decentralize, dematerialize and define.

1. A **defensive strategy** can take on many forms, the most obvious of which is to insure against catastrophe, whatever form that may take. This only works if the crash is not systemic, but it is a good start. Other tactics include having a crack squad of troubleshooters trained to respond in times of crisis, and building up reserves for the proverbial rainy day, which may turn out to be a tsunami.

2. A **diversification strategy** applies to people, products and markets. For example, if you bet your corporate life on being a fossil fuel company, rather than an energy company, or if you are locked into a local market without any global investments, you are highly vulnerable. Likewise, if you hire an army of employee clones, your lack of diversity will leave you brittle in the face of change.

3. A **decentralization strategy** is based on the same rationale that inspired the Internet. By decentralizing information and building in redundancy on local servers, the Internet is far less vulnerable to being taken out in a single hit. In the same way, by decentralizing operations, infrastructure and solutions—as with decentralized energy for example—we can be better prepared to cope with disruption.

4. A **dematerialization strategy** means moving to an industrial model that reduces dependence on resources. The only viable way to do this in the long term is to shift to renewable energy and to optimize the circular economy. Hence, anything we can do to decouple economic growth from environmental impacts is a step in the direction of greater resilience.

5. A **defining strategy** is about giving people a purpose to believe in. Victor Frankl, survivor of four Nazi concentration camps and psychiatric author of *Man's Search for Meaning* (Frankl, 2006), gives compelling evidence that our resilience under extreme circumstances often comes down to having an existential belief about something worth living for. Can sustainability offer us this compelling cause?

By pursing these five resilience strategies, individuals, organizations and even countries will be much better placed to endure the creative destruction to come. However, preparing for change is not the same thing as surviving it. Resilience is not a strategy, but an ability—one which is shaped and tempered in the fire of extreme experience.

At its heart, this ability to be resilient is about adapting when everything around us is changing—like an aspen tree. Aspen forests are able to survive frequent avalanches that literally flatten them. The trees survive and spring back up because they have an interconnected network of underground roots and their trunks and branches are highly pliable.

This brings us back full circle to the message of my introductory chapter on unlocking change, namely that the secret to transformational change in the world is connectivity—to which we can now add that dexterity is also absolutely critical. After all, Darwin never claimed that the fittest would survive, only the most adaptable.

Epilogue: connecting Earth and sky

The birth and rebirth of creation

I want to finish this book by returning to the big picture. Because sustainability is not just about business, leadership and innovation. And it is certainly not just about surviving the future. It is also about living in a world of abundance and diversity in a way that brings joy and inspiration. Jean M. Russell calls this *Thrivability* (Russell, 2013).

When I think about the bigger picture of sustainable frontiers, there are three ideas or questions which come to mind:

First, it is the story of creation—how did the Earth and sky come to exist in the first place, and how do they fit into the grander scheme of things? Second, there are the social and environmental issues surrounding our earth and sky—what impact are we having on our planet and society, for better or for worse? Third, how does Nature influence and inspire us? What are the deeper connections which exist between the living creation which surrounds us and of which we are a part, and our spiritual experience of life?

Let me begin this ending, therefore, by looking at our relationship as human beings with Life. In one African creation myth, as told by Credo Mutwa, Zulu *sangoma* (healer) and *sanusi* (keeper of the legends), the first great nation of human beings were born from the awkward embrace between the Great Mother, *Ninhavanhu-Ma*, or simply *Ma*, and *Simakade*, the Tree of Life. Following their birth the strangest change came over the Tree of Life:

> Green buds burst forth from his writhing limbs and clouds of seeds emerged and fell upon the rocky plains. Soon, all manner of plants and mighty forests grew forth—a creeping carpet of lush living green. From Simakade's roots came reptiles, crawling and slithering, and insects, humming and whining upwards in continuous streams. From his branches dropped snarling, howling, animal fruit, which fell to the ground with a thump and scampered off into the forests in their millions. From great cracks in the trunk of the Tree, birds of all kinds came flying and waddling forth, filling the air with all their love calls.
>
> The earth, which had hitherto been lifeless and dead, began to live, and sounds of all kinds resounded from the forests and valleys, as beast fought beast, beast called beast, and birds sang their happiness loudly towards the smiling sun. The Song of Life had begun on earth—the Song which is still being sung.

Yes, indeed, the Song of Life continues even today. But over the past 100 years or so, there has been an increasing dissonance in that Song, as our human society has caused serious injustices and degradation to the environment. This deals with my second question, namely how we impact on the Earth and Sky.

We have become like the legendary monkeys who, according to one African story, were placed by the great Earth Mother goddess on a sacred fig tree to guard it. They developed such appetites that they not only ate all the figs but also devoured the bark and the wood of the tree. When the great Earth Mother returned, she found the tree reduced to a rotting stump and the skeletons of all the monkeys who had died of starvation after eating their own tree.

So this is the bad news, which we ignore at our peril. Deforestation, climate change, poverty, desertification, inequality, resource depletion, religious intolerance, the collapse of fishing stocks, bribery and corruption, water wars, forced migration and pollution-related disease—these are all critical issues which threaten life as we know it and the very survival of our species and many others. If you think this sounds overly dramatic, well, ignorance is bliss. I could shock you with countless frightening statistics, but instead, I would like to cite a short quotation, taken from *Time Magazine*, about a day in the life of a Child of the Future, assuming we do not change our behaviour:

> The young boy awoke on a hot, oppressive morning. It wasn't a school day, so he could afford to lie back for a while with his favourite storybook. That was the one with drawings of the great forests—the woodlands filled with tall trees, wild animals and clear-running streams. The scenes seemed so magical that the boy could hardly believe

in them, though his parents assured him that such wonders once existed. Closing his book, he saw no joy in the day ahead. He wished the air conditioner weren't broken. He wished there was more food in the refrigerator. He wished he could see the great forests. But there was no use in thinking about that now. It was enough of a struggle just to be alive, especially for a child. (Sancton, 1989)

Recalling and retelling the stories of hope

Even today, this is not as far-fetched as it may seem. But this is a future we want to avoid, so what are the positive signs—the stories of hope? Allow me to share the testimony of four people. They are Edgar Mitchell, James Lovelock (1979), Victor Frankl (2006) and George Washington Carver. And this is why.

Edgar Mitchell, as some of you know, was one of the world's first astronauts to orbit the Earth and walk on the moon. The power of this achievement to change our thinking lay not in his physical journey into space, as incredible as that feat was. Rather, it was the images of our beautiful, fragile, blue-green planet Earth from space, which those first astronauts beamed back to us and captured in countless breathtaking photographs that brought a new consciousness to humanity.

For the first time, we became aware of the Earth as a single, unified, living whole, rather than a politically divided patchwork of countries and societies fighting over resources and money. Edgar Mitchell's account of the affect of these images on him are truly moving. He describes the experience as one equivalent to enlightenment or a revelation, a shift in his being which touched him on a deeply spiritual level. I think this powerful image of the living, unified earth is our first true cause for hope—it is a symbol of both a current physical reality and a future social and spiritual reality to aspire towards.

Then there is James Lovelock (1979), an astronomical scientist who applied science to back up our intuitive understanding of the Earth as a living whole. Lovelock had, since 1965, been working for NASA on a model to determine whether life could exist on Mars or not. In order to do this, he had to ask the question: What are the conditions that sustain life on Earth? But in the course of this investigation, an unexpected conclusion was reached. Namely, that the Earth, previously accepted by science to be an inert, physical object, appears to demonstrate the capacity to self-regulate innumerable conditions (for example, gas concentrations, climate, bacteria growth, etc.) in order to create a suitable environment for life to flourish. And yet this is the very same characteristic which defines living organisms.

His rationale, backed by a rigorous scientific model, was launched to the world in the 1970s as the "Gaia Hypothesis" (Lovelock, 1979), named after the Greek goddess of the Earth. Essentially, the scientific community now had to face up to the challenging fact that the Earth system as a whole may be a living, self-regulating, self-sustaining organism. And yet this is exactly the understanding implied for thousands of years through the mythological images of indigenous cultures, such as the Tree of Life and the Mother Earth Goddess.

Let me move on now to my third question, namely how we are influenced or inspired by Nature. And this is where my third source of hope comes in— Victor Frankl. I have already mentioned that Frankl was a survivor of the Nazi concentration camps and the creator of the psychiatric technique known as Logotherapy, which deals with the way in which people find meaning or purpose in their lives. Frankl, in his book, *Man's Search for Meaning* (Frankl, 2006), gives me great hope about the innate quality in humans to appreciate and be inspired by Nature, even in the direst of circumstances such as those in which he found himself during the Second World War. Here is a quote from his book to illustrate my point:

> As the inner life of the prisoner tended to become more intense, he also experienced the beauty of art and nature as never before. Under their influence he sometimes even forgot his own frightful circumstances. If someone had seen our faces on the [train] journey from Auschwitz to a Bavarian camp as we beheld the mountains of Salzburg with their summits glowing in the sunset, through the little barred windows of the prison carriage, he would never have believed that those were the faces of men who had given up hope on all life and liberty. Despite that factor—or maybe because of it—we were carried away by nature's beauty, which we had missed for so long.
>
> In camp too, a man might draw the attention of a comrade working next to him to a nice view of the setting sun shining through the tall trees of the Bavarian woods, the same woods in which we had built an enormous, hidden munitions plant. One evening, when we were already resting on the floor of our hut, dead tired, soup bowls in hand, a fellow prisoner rushed in and asked us to run out to the assembly grounds and see the wonderful sunset. Standing outside we saw sinister clouds glowing in the west and the whole sky alive with clouds of ever-changing shapes and colours, from steel blue to blood red. The desolate grey mud huts provided a sharp contrast, while the puddles on the muddy ground reflected the glowing sky. Then, after minutes

of moving silence, one prisoner said to another, "How beautiful the world *could* be!"

Frankl (2006) also gives us a clue to why we may be in the collective state of abusing our planet, much in the same way as they were abused as prisoners in the concentration camps. He talks about how, on their day of release from the camp, they all went walking in a meadow close-by filled with flowers. But to their surprise, they felt almost incapable of appreciating its beauty. They had become numb to beauty and experiencing pleasure.

Could this not be the same mental state in which our city-bound, rat-race-stressed population of today finds themselves? Many people have become so isolated and detached from Nature that they feel numb—incapable of sensing its beauty and wonder, and insensitive to any damage they may be causing it.

Relearning the skill of listening to life

A final clue comes from the last, perhaps least known, person I mentioned earlier, namely George Washington Carver, an American slave descendant who became known as the "Black Leonardo". Were it not for his achievements, Carver would probably have been written off by history as one of those crazy, uneducated, superstitious, but harmless, mumbo-jumbo types. Why? Because he talked to, listened to, sang to and healed plants.

But the world could not ignore him, for Carver was an agricultural chemist with a Masters degree who discovered the commercial benefits of the peanut (used only for hog food at the time around the Civil War) and the sweet potato. In his long career which stretched into his eighties, Carver invented hundreds of new products—including cosmetics, axle grease, printers' ink, petroleum substitutes, shampoos, creosote, vinegar and wood stains, to mention but a few. All from nature's bounty. And all because he took the time to listen to nature's wisdom. When asked about his prolific knowledge and inventions, he had this to say:

> Nature is the greatest teacher and I learn from her best when others are asleep. In the still dark hours before sunrise, God tells me of the plans I am to fulfil ... The secrets are in the plants. To elicit them you have to love them enough ... Everyone can, if only they believe it. (Clark, 2011)

And indeed, perhaps the world is beginning to learn from Carver. For most of the world's newest and fastest developing technologies do nothing more than attempt to mimic the ingenuity of nature, from artificial intelligence and bio-technologies, to solar energy and phototronics.

But what about each of us in our own daily lives. Are we listening? I believe that, for Creation to be healed, each of us needs to be that connection between Earth and Sky. We each need to find our own sense of meaning and inspiration from nature—whether by growing things, walking in the mountains and forests, actively campaigning for environmental issues, consciously buying fair-trade and environmentally friendly products, or allowing ourselves to relate more intimately with the people and creatures which share our planet.

There is a useful little way to maintain a focus on this process of listening and learning from nature. Most ancient indigenous cultures have a strong tradition of animal, plant or landscape totems. We should not treat these as superstitious nonsense, for we create our own meaning, and most meaning can be found in symbols. Ask yourself: Which of nature's creations most inspires, teaches or challenges you? "Adopt" a particular animal, or tree, or river, or mountain, or sea, and learn as much as you can from it, before looking for a new totem.

In my own life, I stumbled across the fairly unlikely influence and wonder of geese, after a close encounter with two birds that flew past me when I was at Zoo Lake in Johannesburg many years ago. And to illustrate how meaning can emerge from a totemic relationship with another creature, this is what I learned about geese:

The goose was the sacred bird in Rome's temple of Juna and was associated with Boreas, the North Wind in Greek Mythology. It is also the totem for the winter solstice in the Native American medicine wheel. The goose is symbolic of writing and storytelling, with its quill having been used as a pen for many generations. In more practical terms, by flying together in V-formation, geese get where they are going almost twice as quickly with half the effort. When the lead goose gets tired, it simply drops to the back of the formation and another takes the lead. Those near the back continually honk encouragement to the ones upfront. And when one of the geese is injured or becomes ill and drops out of the formation, two other geese always drop out and stay with it until it recovers.

The spirit of the goose has continued to inspire me. In fact, I have written a book on leadership (as yet unpublished) in which Gulliver, a Scottish goose, gets lost on his way to Leadership School in London, and ends up travelling down through Africa learning unusual lessons in leadership. The book is called: *Follow Me! (I'm Lost): The Tale of an Unexpected Leader.*

So what is your messenger from Nature? Are you ready to listen? Carver summed up the essence of this vital ability:

> When I touch that flower, I am touching infinity. It existed long before there were human beings on earth and will to continue to exist for millions of years to come. Through the flower, I talk to the Infinite, which is only a silent force. This is not a physical contact. It is not an earthquake, wind or fire. It is in the invisible world. It is that still small voice that calls up the fairies. Many people know this instinctively.

So perhaps, if we listen to our hearts and our souls, if we tune in to the Earth Spirit, we can help to ensure that the Child of the Future, quoted in *Time Magazine*, faces this far happier prospect:

> The young girl awoke on a cool, inviting morning. It wasn't a school day, so she could look forward to doing what she liked best. Her family was going just outside the city into the great forest, where they would stroll under the tall trees, spot wild animals and wade in the clear-running streams.
>
> Every time they went, she felt lucky. After all, her parents had told her stories about the old days—before people learned to protect the land and water and harness the power of wind and sunlight. It was a dark time when the forests died, rivers ran dry and millions went hungry. The girl was amazed and frightened that such a thing could ever have happened. But there was no need to think about that now—not with a glorious day ahead. It was so good to be alive, especially for a child. (Sancton, 1989)

References

Abo Sena, A. (2014). Case study: promotion of eco-innovation in SMEs from the chemicals sector. Presentation to the UNEP-UNIDO expert review meeting on eco-industrial parks and technology and eco-innovation, Vienna, May 5–7.

Accenture & UN Global Compact (2010). A new era of sustainability: UN Global Compact–Accenture CEO study 2010. Report. New York: Accenture & UN Global Compact.

Alacero (2014). Latin America in figures 2013. Report. Santiago: Latin American Steel Association.

Ancona, D., & Backman, E. (2010). It's not all about you. *Harvard Business Review*, April 26.

Anderson, C. (2006). *The Long Tail: Why the Future of Business is Selling Less of More*. New York: Hyperion Books.

Arthur, C. (2006). What's the 1% rule? *The Guardian*, 20 July.

Bach, R. (1977). *Illusions: The Adventures of a Reluctant Messiah*. London: William Heinemann.

Bakan, J. (2004). *The Corporation: The Pathological Pursuit of Profit and Power*. New York: Simon & Schuster.

Barton, D., & Wiseman, M. (2014). Focusing capital on the long term. *Harvard Business Review*, January.

Baue, B. & Murninghan, M. (2010) The accountability web: weaving corporate accountability and interactive technology. CSR Initiative Working Paper, No. 58. Boston: Harvard University.

BBMG, Globescan & SustainAbility (2012). Re:Thinking consumption. Report. London: BBMG.

Beavan, C. (2011). *No Impact Man: Saving the Planet One Family at a Time*. London: Piatkus.

Beckhard, R., & Harris, R.T. (1987). *Organizational Transitions: Understanding Complex Change*. London: Addison-Wesley.

Beek, K. (2012). Interview with Krispijn Beek, CSR manager at Strukton, conducted by Wayne Visser, director of Kaleidoscope Futures.

Benkler, Y. (2006). *The Wealth of Networks: How Social Production Transforms Markets and Freedom*. New York: Yale University Press.

Benyus, J. (1997). *Biomimicry: Innovation Inspired by Nature*. New York: William Morris.

Blakeman, C. (2014). Why "participation age" leaders will beat old-school managers, every time. *Inc.*, September 2.

Boulding, K.E. (1966) The economics of the coming spaceship earth. In H. Jarrett (Ed.), *Environmental Quality in a Growing Economy* (pp. 3-14). Baltimore, MD: Resources for the Future/Johns Hopkins University Press.

Bowen, H.R. (1953). *Social Responsibilities of the Businessman*. Iowa City: University of Iowa Press.

Braungart, M., & McDonough, W. (2008). *Cradle to Cradle: Remaking the Way We Make Things*. London: Jonathan Cape.

Brunswick (2013). The future of stakeholder engagement. Report. New York: Brunswick.

Bureau of International Recycling (2014). World steel recycling in figures. Report. Brussels: BIR.

Capra, F. (1982). *The Turning Point: Science, Society and the Rising Culture*. New York: Simon & Schuster.

Carberry, E. (2012). Interview with Elle Carberry, co-founder and managing director of the China Greentech Initiative, conducted by Wayne Visser, director of Kaleidoscope Futures.

Carroll, A.B. (1991). The pyramid of corporate social responsibility: toward the moral management of organizational stakeholders. *Business Horizons*, 34:39-48.

Carroll, L. (1865). *Alice's Adventures in Wonderland*. London: William Collins.

Carson, N. (2010). Interview with Neil Carson, CEO of Johnson Matthey, conducted by Polly Courtice, director of Cambridge Institute for Sustainability Leadership.

Carson, R. (1962). *Silent Spring*. Boston, MA: Houghton Mifflin.

Chekhov, A.P. (1995). *The Bet*. Sydney: HarperCollins Publishers Australia.

Cheshire, I. (2010). Interview with Ian Cheshire, CEO of Kingfisher, conducted by Polly Courtice, director of Cambridge Institute for Sustainability Leadership.

Clark, G. (2011). *The Man Who Talks with the Flowers: The Intimate Life Story of Dr George Washington Carver*. Eastford, CT: Martino Fine Books.

Clean Edge (2014). Clean energy trends 2014. Report.

Confino, J. (2012). Ben & Jerry's: parent companies don't always know best. *The Guardian*, October 22.

Corporate Leadership Council (2004). Driving performance and retention through employee engagement. Report. London: Corporate Leadership Council.

Corporate Sustainability Reporting Coalition (2013). Briefing paper. April. London: Corporate Sustainability Reporting Coalition.

Dalla Costa, J. (1991). *Meditations on Business: Why Business as Usual Won't Work Anymore*. Toronto: Prentice Hall Canada.

Diamond, J. (2005). *Collapse: How Societies Choose to Fail or Survive*. London: Allen Lane.

Dolan, C.S., & Opondo, M. (2005). Seeking common ground: multi-stakeholder processes in Kenya's cut flower industry. *Journal of Corporate Citizenship*, No. 18, April.

Doppelt, B. (2012). *From Me to We: The Five Transformational Commitments Required to Rescue the Planet, Your Organization, and Your Life*. Sheffield: Greenleaf Publishing.

Drucker, P. (1959). *The Landmarks of Tomorrow*. London: Heinemann.

Ecofys (2010). World GHG Emissions Flow Chart. London: Ecofys.

Ecorys (2012). Mapping resource prices: the past and the future. Report. Rotterdam: Ecorys.

Ehrlich, P. (1968). *The Population Bomb*. New York: Ballantine Books.

Elkington, J. (2012). *Zeronauts: Breaking the Sustainability Barrier*. London: Routledge.

Elkington, J., & Hartigan, P. (2008). *The Power of Unreasonable People*. Boston, MA: Harvard Business School Press.

European Commission. (2011). Boosting green business. Brussels: Executive Agency for Competitiveness and Innovation of the European Commission.

EY (2013). Six growing trends in corporate sustainability. Report. London: Ernst & Young.

—— (2014). RECAI: Renewable energy country attractiveness index. Issue 40, February. London: Ernst & Young.

Ferguson, M. (1982). *The Aquarian Conspiracy: Personal and Social Transformation in Our Time*. New York: Granada Publishing.

Frankl, V.E. (2006). *Man's Search for Meaning*. Boston, MA: Beacon Press.

Gore, A. (2007). *An Inconvenient Truth: The Planetary Emergency of Global Warming and What We Can Do About it*. Logan, IA: Perfection Learning.

Grant Thornton (2013). The Grant Thornton international business report. November. London: Grant Thornton.

GRI (2009). Trends in online sustainability reporting. Report. Amsterdam: Global Reporting Initiative.

Handy, C. (1998). *The Hungry Spirit: Beyond Capitalism—A Quest for Purpose in the Modern World*. London: Random House.

Harman, W. (1980). *Global Mind Change: The New Age Revolution in the Way We Think*. New York: Warner Books.

Hartman, P. (2013). Interview with Petra Hartman, project officer at Ekvilib Institute, conducted by Wayne Visser, director of Kaleidoscope Futures.

Hawken, P. (1993). *The Ecology of Commerce*. London: HarperBusiness.

Hawken, P., Lovins, A., & Lovins, L.H. (1999). *Natural Capitalism: Creating the Next Industrial Revolution*. New York: Little Brown and Company.

Heinberg, R. (2007). *Peak Everything: Waking Up to the Century of Decline in Earth's Resources*. West Hoathly: Clairview Books.

Henderson, D. (2001). *Misguided Virtue: False Notions of Corporate Social Responsibility*. Auckland: New Zealand Business Roundtable.

Henderson, H. (1993). *Paradigms in Progress: Life Beyond Economics*. San Francisco: Berrett-Koehler.

Hikisch, D. (2013). Interview with Dermot Hikisch, B Lab's head of community development, conducted by Wayne Visser, director of Kaleidoscope Futures.

Immelt, J. (2007). GE's Jeff Immelt on the 10 keys to great leadership. Fast Company, December 19.

Kaleidoscope Futures (2015). Transforming corporate accountability: the revolutions of transparency, ratings and social media. Report. London: Kaleidoscope Futures.

Kinsman, F. (1990). *Millennium: Towards Tomorrow's Society*. London: W.H. Allen.

Kohn, A. (1993). *No Contest: The Case Against Competition*. New York: Houghton Mifflin.

KPMG (2013). Carrots and sticks: sustainability reporting policies worldwide—today's best practice, tomorrow's trends. Report. Amsterdam: KPMG.

—— (2014). 2014 KPMG survey of corporate responsibility reporting. Report. Amsterdam: KPMG.

Kuhn, T. (1962). *The Structure of Scientific Revolutions*. Chicago: University of Chicago Press.

Kuslan, A.K. (2013). Interview with Ales Kranjc Kuslan, director of Ekvilib Institute, conducted by Wayne Visser, director of Kaleidoscope Futures.

Kymal, C., Gruska, G., & Reid, R.D. (2015). *Integrated Management Systems*. Milwaukee: ASQ Quality Press.

Lievegoed, B. (1991). *Managing the Developing Organization: Tapping the Spirit of Europe*. London: Wiley-Blackwell.

Lopez, I. (2012). Interview with Itzel Lopez of the IDEARSE centre, conducted by Wayne Visser, director of Kaleidoscope Futures.

Lopez, J. (2010). Interview with José Lopez, executive vice president Operations and GLOBE of Nestlé, conducted by Polly Courtice, director of Cambridge Institute for Sustainability Leadership.

Lovelock, J. (1979). *Gaia: A New Look at Life on Earth*. Oxford: Oxford University Press.

Maslow, A. (1954). *Motivation and Personality*. New York: Joanna Cotler Books.

—— (1965). *Eupsychian Management*. Homewood, IL: R.D. Irwin.

—— (1971). *The Farther Reaches of Human Nature*. New York: Viking Press.

Matten, D., & Moon, J. (2008). "Implicit" and "explicit" CSR: a conceptual framework for a comparative understanding of corporate social responsibility. *Academy of Management Review*, Vol. 33, No. 2, 404-424.

McElhaney, K.A., & Mobasseri, S. (2012). Women create a sustainable future. Report. San Francisco: UC Berkeley Haas School of Business.

McGregor, D. (1960). *The Human Side of Enterprise*. New York: McGraw Hill Higher Education.

McKinsey (2011). Resource revolution: meeting the world's energy, materials, food, and water needs. Report. New York: McKinsey & Co.

—— (2013). Ten IT-enabled business trends for the decade ahead. Report. New York: McKinsey & Co.

Meza, I. (2013). Interview with Isabel Meza, head of integrated management at Adelca, conducted by Wayne Visser, director of Kaleidoscope Futures

Millennium Ecosystem Assessment (2005). *Ecosystems and Human Well-Being: Synthesis Report*. Washington, DC: Island Press.

Miller, J., & Parker, L. (2013). *Everybody's Business*. London: Biteback Publishing.

Mintzberg, H. (1976). Planning on the left side and managing the right. *Harvard Business Review*, July.

Morozov, E. (2009). The brave new world of slacktivism. *Foreign Policy*, May 19.

Moss Kanter, R. (1989). *When Giants Learn to Dance: Mastering the Challenges of Strategy, Management and Careers in the 1990s*. New York: Simon & Schuster.

Muehlfeit, J. (2010). Interview with Jan Muehlfeit, chairman of Microsoft Europe, conducted by Polly Courtice, director of Cambridge Institute for Sustainability Leadership.

Musk, E. (2011). Interview with Elon Musk, CEO of SpaceX and Tesla Motors, conducted by Lincoln P. Bloomfield, Jr, Chairman of the Board, Henry L. Stimson Center.

Nalebuff, B., & Brandenburger, A. (1996). *Co-opetition*. New York: HarperCollins.

Nash, T. (2012). Global green R&D report. Toronto: Centre for Social Innovation, August 29.

NCDPPEA (2009) Water efficiency: industry specific processes—metal finishing. Report. Raleigh, NC: North Carolina Division of Pollution Prevention and Environmental Assistance (NCDPPEA).

O'Connor, C. (2013). New app lets you boycott Koch Brothers, Monsanto and more by scanning your shopping cart. *Forbes*, May 14.

Pearce, F. (2006). *When the Rivers Run Dry: What Happens When Our Water Runs Out?* London: Eden Project Books.

Philips, O. (1979). A new course for management. In J. Fabry, R. Bulka, & W. Sahakian (Eds.), *Logotherapy in Action* (pp. 4-11). New York: Jason Aronson.

PleaseCycle (2012). Introduction pack. Report. London: PleaseCycle.

Porritt, J. (2013). *The World We Made: Alex McKay's Story from 2050*. London: Phaidon Press.

Porter, M.E., & Kramer, M.R. (2011). Creating shared value. *Harvard Business Review*, January.

Prahalad, C.K., & Hart, S.L. (2002). The fortune at the bottom of the pyramid. *Strategy+Business*, No. 26, First quarter.

Roddick, A. (2005). *Business As Unusual: My Entrepreneurial Journey, Profits with Principles*. London: Anita Roddick Books.

Russell, J.M. (2013). *Thrivability: Breaking Through to a World That Works*. Axminster: Triarchy Press.

Russell, P. (1984). *The Awakening Earth: The Global Brain*. London: Ark.

Salman, M., Koohafkan, P., & Casarotto, C. (2010). Investments in land and water. SOLAW Background Thematic Report TR17. Rome: FAO.

Sancton, T.A. (1989). Planet of the year: what on EARTH are we doing? *Time Magazine*, January 2.

Schuurman, M. (2012). Interview with Michel Schuurman, a director at MVO Nederland, conducted by Wayne Visser, director of Kaleidoscope Futures.

Semler, R. (1993). *Maverick: The Success Story Behind the World's Most Unusual Workplace*. New York: Century.

Senge, P. (2006). *The Fifth Discipline: The Art and Practice of the Learning Organization*. 2nd edition. London: Random House Business.

Siegel, D. (2010). *Pull: The Power of the Semantic Web to Transform Your Business*. London: Penguin Putnam.

Sim, J. (2011). *Simple Jack*. Singapore: Straits Times Press.

Smith, A. (1982). *The Wealth of Nations*. London: Penguin Classics.

Smuts, J.C. (1926). *Holism and Evolution*. Gouldsboro, ME: Gestalt Journal Press.

Spence, L. (2012). Interview with Laura Spence, director of the Royal Holloway University of London's Centre for Research into Sustainability, conducted by Wayne Visser, director of Kaleidoscope Futures.

SS-GATE (2010). 2010 SS-GATE convention held in Shanghai. Report. Shanghai: South-South Global Assets and Technology Exchange (SS-GATE).

Strom, S. (2014). Nestle moves toward humane treatment of animals at its supplier. *New York Times*, 20 August.

SustainAbility (2010). Rate the raters: phase two—taking inventory of the ratings universe. Report. London: SustainAbility.

—— (2011a). Signed, sealed ... delivered? Report. London: SustainAbility.

—— (2011b). Web 2.0 survey. Report. London: SustainAbility.

—— (2013). Rate the raters: phase five—the raters' response. Report. London: SustainAbility.

Sustainly (2013). Social media sustainability index 2013. Report. Cardiff: Sustainly.

Sustrans (2012). The real cycling revolution: how the face of cycling is changing. Report. Bristol: Sustrans.

Tapscott, D., & Williams, A.D. (2007). *Wikinomics: How Mass Collaboration Changes Everything*. London: Atlantic Books.

Toynbee, A.J. (1988). *A Study of History*. Oxford: Oxford University Press.

UNDP (2006). Fast facts: the faces of poverty. New York: UN Millennium Project

UNEP (2011). Recycling rates of metals. Report. Nairobi: United Nations Environment Programme.

—— (2015). Moving ahead with technologies for eco-innovation. Report. Nairobi: United Nations Environment Programme. Prepared by Wayne Visser and due for publication in 2015.

UNEP & Öko-Institut (2009). Critical metals for future sustainable technologies and their recycling potential. Report. Nairobi: United Nations Environment Programme.

Useful Social Media (2013). State of social corporate media. Report. London: Useful Social Media.

Utopies (2012). Sustainability reporting at a cross roads. Report. Paris: Utopies.

van Dalen, M. (2012). Interview with Mariska van Dalen, a circular economy expert at the consultancy and engineering firm Tebodin, conducted by Wayne Visser, director of Kaleidoscope Futures.

Visser, W. (2008). *Making A Difference: Purpose-Inspired Leadership for Corporate Sustainability and Responsibility (CSR)*. Saarbrücken: VDM Verlag Dr. Müller.

—— (2011). *The Age of Responsibility: CSR 2.0 and the New DNA of Business*. London: Wiley.

—— (2013). *CSR 2.0: Transforming Corporate Sustainability and Responsibility*. London: Springer.

—— (2014). *Follow Me! (I'm Lost): The Tale of an Unexpected Leader*. Unpublished.

Visser, W., & Courtice, P. (2011). Sustainability leadership: linking theory and practice. *SSRN Paper Series*, October 21, 2011. Available at: http://ssrn.com/abstract=1947221.

Visser, W. & CPSL (2009). *The Top 50 Sustainability Books*. For Cambridge Programme for Sustainability Leadership (CPSL). Sheffield: Greenleaf Publishing.

Visser, W., & Sunter, C. (2002). *Beyond Reasonable Greed: Why Sustainable Business is a Much Better Idea!* Cape Town: Tafelberg Human & Rousseau.

Visser, W., Matten, D., Pohl, M., & Tolhurst, N. (2007). *The A to Z of Corporate Social Responsibility: A Complete Reference Guide to Concepts, Codes and Organisations.* London: Wiley.

Volans & GRI (2010). The transparent economy. Report. London: Volans.

Waterman Jr, R.H., & Peters, T. (1985). *In Search of Excellence: Lessons from America's Best-Run Companies.* New York: Harper and Row.

Weber Shandwick/KRC Research (2010). Crowdsourcing and social media: a survey of business executives. Report. New York: Weber Shandwick.

Wheeler, D., & Sillanpää, M. (1997). *The Stakeholder Corporation: A Blueprint for Maximizing Stakeholder Value.* Harlow: Financial Times/Prentice Hall.

White, A. (2012). Redefining value: the future of corporate sustainability ratings. IFC, *Private Sector Opinion, 29.*

World Economic Forum (2009). Driving sustainable consumption: closed loop systems. Report. Geneva: World Economic Forum.

—— (2012). Global Agenda Council on Emerging Technologies issue brief. Report. Geneva: World Economic Forum.

World Steel Association (2014). World in steel 2014. Report. Brussels: World Steel Association.

Yeomans, M. (2013). Why crowdsourcing should become part of a company's DNA. *Guardian Sustainable Business* blog, February.

Zadek, S. (2001). *The Civil Corporation.* London: Earthscan Publications.

Content sources

The following is a list of references to where content in this book was first published.

Introduction

Visser, W. (2013). The sustainability movement faces extinction—what could save it? *The Guardian*, September 30.

Chapter 1: Unlocking change through transformational leadership

Visser, W. (2013). Finding your inner sustainability superhero. *The Guardian*, October 21.
—— (2013). Systems change requires multiple agents and dynamics. *The Guardian*, October 7.
—— (2013). To survive in a volatile world businesses must build in resilience. *The Guardian*, October 28.
—— (2013). Unlock change with big beliefs, blue skies, burning platforms and baby steps. *The Guardian*, October 14.
—— (2014). Overcoming the barriers to sustainable change. *The Guardian*, January 21.
—— (2015). Seven ways to test if your leader is fit for the future. *The Guardian*, forthcoming.
Visser, W., & Sunter, C. (2002). Beyond reasonable greed: from accounting to accountability. *Accountancy SA*, September.

Chapter 2: Unlocking change through enterprise reform

Visser, W. (1994). New paradigms in business: the power of perception. *HRM*, October.
—— (2012). Family friendly enterprise: Slovenia leads the way. *The Guardian*, October 1.
—— (2012). Practising social responsibility without the CSR label. *The Guardian*, September 12.
—— (2012). Water footprints: lessons from Kenya's floriculture sector. *The Guardian*, August 20.
—— (2012). Where next for the circular economy? *The Guardian*, December 10.
—— (2012). Women and sustainability: taking a lead in China. *The Guardian*, October 26.

—— (2013). Can legal reforms rescue business back from greedy shareholders? *The Guardian*, February 22.

—— (2013). Cycling is sustainable and healthy so why aren't more of us on our bikes? *The Guardian*, 20 June.

Chapter 3: Unlocking change through technology innovation

Visser, W. (2014). 8 lessons from Egypt in building a cleaner chemicals industry. *The Guardian*, October 8.

—— (2014). Closing the loop on steel: what we can learn from a manufacturer in Ecuador. *The Guardian*, November 20.

—— (2014). Eco-innovation: going beyond creating technology for technology's sake. *The Guardian*, December 4.

—— (2014). How to use technology to make our planet more sustainable, not less. *The Guardian*, July 16.

—— (2014). Iron ore and rare earth metals mining: an industry under siege? *The Guardian*, October 24.

—— (2014). Meeting water and energy challenges in the agri-food sector with technology. *The Guardian*, August 13.

—— (2014). Sustainable tech in Africa: 10 lessons from a cassava company. *The Guardian*, August 26.

—— (2014). Tackling the food waste challenge with technology. *The Guardian*, July 29.

—— (2014). Why banning dangerous chemicals is not enough. *The Guardian*, September 16.

—— (2014). Why metals should be recycled, not mined. *The Guardian*, November 4.

—— (2014). Will green chemistry save us from toxification? *The Guardian*, September 24.

Chapter 4: Unlocking change through corporate transparency

Kaleidoscope Futures (2015). Transforming corporate accountability: the revolutions of transparency, ratings and social media. Report. London: Kaleidoscope Futures.

Chapter 5: Unlocking change through stakeholder engagement

Kaleidoscope Futures (2015). Transforming corporate accountability: the revolutions of transparency, ratings and social media. Report. London: Kaleidoscope Futures.

Chapter 6: Unlocking change through social responsibility

Visser, W. (2010). The age of responsibility: CSR 2.0 and the new DNA of business. *Journal of Business Systems, Governance and Ethics*, Vol. 5, No. 3, p. 7.

—— (2012). CSR 2.0: reinventing corporate social responsibility for the 21st century. *Management Innovation eXchange*, May 13.

—— (2013). Personal reflections on responsible competitiveness. *CSR & Competitiveness*, July.

Chapter 7: Unlocking change through integrated value

Visser, W. (1995). Holism: a new framework for thinking about business. *New Perspectives*, No. 7.

—— (2003). Meaning, work and social responsibility. *Positive Living E-Zine*, International Network on Personal Meaning, September.

—— (2013). Creating shared value: revolution or clever con? *The Broker Online*, June 17.

—— (2015). Creating integrated value: beyond CSR and CSV to CIV. *The Journal of International Business Ethics*, forthcoming.

Chapter 8: Unlocking change through future-fitness

Visser, W. (1993). Beyond the Information Age: in search of new images of the future. *New Paradigms*, No. 4.

—— (2012). A test for future fitness: make it safe, smart, shared, sustainable and satisfying. *Kaleidoscope Futures Inspiration Series*, No. 1.

—— (2013). Visions of the future: CSR, sustainable business and capitalism in 2020. *CSRwire*, September 10.

Epilogue: connecting Earth and sky

Visser, W. (2001). Connecting earth and sky. *Namaste*, Vol. 14, November/December.

About the author

Dr Wayne Visser is Director of the think-tank Kalei-doscope Futures, Founder of CSR International and Vice President of Sustainability Services for Omnex Inc. In addition, Wayne is Chair of Sustainable Business at the Gordon Institute of Business Science in South Africa, Adjunct Professor of Sustainable Development at Deakin Business School in Australia and Senior Associate at the University of Cambridge Programme for Sustainability Leadership in the UK.

Wayne is the author of 23 books, including *The CSR International Research Compendium* (2015), *Disrupting the Future* (2014), *CSR 2.0* (2013), *The Quest for Sustainable Business* (2012), *The Age of Responsibility* (2011) and *The World Guide to CSR* (2010). He is a guest columnist for *The Guardian* newspaper and has also published over 300 other works (chapters, articles, etc.). He has delivered more than 250 professional speeches all around the world, with his work taking him to 70 countries in the last 20 years.

Wayne has been listed as one of the Top 100 Influencers on Twitter in Corporate Social Responsibility and Sustainable Business (2014); a Top 100 Thought Leader in Trustworthy Business Behavior (2013); a Top 100 Global Sustain Ability Leader (2012 and 2011); a Top 100 Thought Leader in Europe and the Middle East (2011); a Top 100 CSR Leader and a Top 20 Sustainability Leader (2012 and 2009). He is also the recipient of the Global CSR Excellence and Leadership Award (2013), the Emerald Literati Outstanding Author Contribution Award (2011) and the Outstanding Teacher Award of the Warwick MBA (2010/11 and 2011/12).

Before getting his PhD in Corporate Social Responsibility (Nottingham University, UK), Wayne was Director of Sustainability Services for KPMG and Strategy Analyst for Cap Gemini in South Africa. His other qualifications include an MSc in Human Ecology (Edinburgh University, UK) and a Bachelor of Business Science with Honours in Marketing (Cape Town University, South Africa).

Wayne lives in Cambridge, UK, and enjoys art, nature, writing poetry and learning about new countries and cultures. A full biography and much of his writing and art is on www.waynevisser.com.

By the same author

Non-fiction

Beyond Reasonable Greed
South Africa: Reasons to Believe
Corporate Citizenship in Africa
Business Frontiers
The A to Z of Corporate Social Responsibility
Making A Difference
Landmarks for Sustainability
The Top 50 Sustainability Books
The World Guide to CSR
The Age of Responsibility
The Quest for Sustainable Business
CSR 2.0
Disrupting the Future
The CSR International Research Compendium

Fiction

I Am an African
Wishing Leaves
Seize the Day
African Dream
String, Donuts, Bubbles and Me
Icarus
Life in Transit